WHEN YOUR CHILD IS GRIEVING

AMY E. FORD
Licensed Professional Counselor

HARVEST HOUSE PUBLISHERS
EUGENE, OREGON

Italicized emphasis in Scripture quotations is added by the author.

Cover design, illustration, and hand lettering by Connie Gabbert Design + Illustration

Cover photo © NikolaVukojevic / iStock

This book includes stories in which people's names and some details of their situations have been changed.

When Your Child Is Grieving

Published by Harvest House Publishers
Eugene, Oregon 97408
www.harvesthousepublishers.com

ISBN 978-0-7369-7595-7 (pbk.)
ISBN 978-0-7369-7596-4 (eBook)

Library of Congress Cataloging-in-Publication Data

Names: Ford, Amy E., author.
Title: When your child is grieving / Amy E. Ford.
Description: Eugene, Oregon : Harvest House Publishers, [2019] | Includes bibliographical references.
Identifiers: LCCN 2018061346 (print) | LCCN 2019001560 (ebook) | ISBN 9780736975964 (ebook) | ISBN 9780736975957 (pbk.)
Subjects: LCSH: Grief in children—Religious aspects—Christianity.
Classification: LCC BV4906 (ebook) | LCC BV4906 .F67 2019 (print) | DDC 248.8/66—dc23
LC record available at https://lccn.loc.gov/2018061346

Printed in the United States of America

19 20 21 22 23 24 25 26 27 / BP-RD / 10 9 8 7 6 5 4 3 2 1

"*When Your Child Is Grieving* provides a helpful balance—recognizing the strength found in our faith while using tools from the mental health community to address this difficult subject. Amy Ford's encouragement, insights, and practical advice give the tools you need to help a child cope with loss. I highly recommend this much-needed resource."

Darlene Brock
author of *Raising Great Girls*
and cohost of *This Girl Parent Life Podcast*

"As a pastor, mother of three, and professional counselor, I found this book to be an oasis in a desert place. *When Your Child Is Grieving* vividly illustrates the devastating darkness of grief in a child's life and shines the light of God's remarkable power to bring hope and healing. This book is a compassionate and strategic guide for parents of grieving children."

Sandra Stubbs
licensed professional counselor and senior pastor

"Dr. Amy Ford has written a book that is both a practical guide to supporting children in grief and a source of inspiration and hope for parents and caregivers. Her words drip with grace and encouragement as she draws from her clinical knowledge and personal experience. I highly recommend this guide for any educator who daily works to support children experiencing grief and loss."

Heidi Brown
elementary school principal

"As a director of a nonprofit benefiting orphans, foster children, and children impacted by family separation, I see firsthand how the burden of grief can traumatize children. *When Your Child Is Grieving* is a relatable, heartfelt resource for caregivers of grieving children. It introduces scientific child-development principles for trauma-informed healing and provides practical guidance and applications to empower those experiencing grief at a young age. The helpful summaries of key points, specific parenting skills, and activities for caregivers to practice with children will promote conversation, growth, and hope. *When Your*

Child Is Grieving is an essential tool for caregivers of grieving children and for young adults who experienced grief at a young age."

Tammy Teske
director of programs, SPOON Foundation

"With compassion and kindness, Amy Ford provides the tools parents need to minister effectively to their grieving, brokenhearted children and to provide the comfort, security, and healing those kids need. I was touched by the way Dr. Ford lays a foundation of grace and spiritual guidance for parents who must nurture their children through times of loss. She also provides a clinically sound approach to applying the wisdom you need. You may even discover some gaps in your own childhood development that have followed you into adulthood. Finding hope for more healing in your own life will greatly enhance your ability to help the child you love so dearly."

Tim Ravan
president, Global Connectors

To children who walk this life with
hollow eyes and broken hearts—children who have
sat at my dining room table, in my classrooms,
and in my counseling office.
I see you, and God sees you too.
Joy and abundance are promised for you.

Acknowledgments

Always first, I acknowledge Jesus Christ, my Savior and Healer. Thanks to you, God, for your words. May you ever be glorified.

To my family, forever my best gift. Thank you for your love and support.

Jesse Kratz and Hannah Adams, thank you for your research assistance. Both of you women are stellar counselors and scholars, and every day you are helping children and families with your compassion and empathy.

To all the people at Harvest House Publishers who helped envision, develop, edit, and otherwise put together this book—I am so very grateful. Heather Green, Hope Lyda, Gene Skinner, and all the rest—copyeditors, cover designers, editors, marketing and sales staff, support staff, and prayer warriors—this project would not have happened without you. You are an amazing team, and I'm so grateful to have you. Thank you for investing in a new author.

To the precious children who shared their hearts through the illustrations in this book, thank you.

Leif Ford and Ev Denniston, two godly men and caring pastors, thank you for your theological guidance.

Contents

He's with the Lord how I see
He's where he's supposed to be
even though he's not with me
he's where he shoud be.
Heaven is a perfect place to be.

Art by Annika, age 9

Begin with the Most Important Thing

God said, "My presence will go with you.
I'll see the journey to the end."

Exodus 33:14 msg

When grief enters your home and touches your child, it is you, the parent or guardian, who bears the primary responsibility of helping that child. You can feel lost and alone in the journey for many reasons.

Sometimes it isn't obvious that grief is the root of a change in a child.

We often associate grief with death, yet any situation of loss can initiate grief in a child—the altering of a family through divorce, a long-term disability or impairment of a family member, a missing pet, moving away from a cherished friend, or growing up in foster care.

Children grieve differently.

You may sense that grief is in the heart of your child, but you might not understand the way it is echoing throughout their life and actions. Some children grieve quietly. They go to school, softball practice, and church, doing what they're supposed to do without anyone ever seeing their broken hearts. Other children grieve loudly. Their grief triggers actions that get noticed and possibly mislabeled as ADHD, oppositional defiance, rebellion, or other unwanted behavior.

We have a hard time talking about grief.

We don't know what to say or how to say it, so we don't say anything at all. And our children continue to grieve. When the thought of writing this book first crossed my mind and planted a seed in my heart, I must admit that my own discomfort about how to approach you and your child's pain held me back. I care deeply. I am a mental health professional, a pastor's wife, and a teacher of counselors—caring for others is what I do every day. Still, I wasn't sure how to enter this conversation with you.

Resources are difficult to find.

Parents and mentors of grieving children don't know where to turn. Soon after the possibility of this book started to grow in my heart, I was preparing a counseling class on crisis, trauma, and grief, and I couldn't find any good sources for helping grieving children. I was at a loss on how to train my counseling students in this area. And that was a problem because counselors encounter so many grieving children at school and in their therapy offices. It became clear that if good resources for counselors are hard to find, then even fewer good resources are available for parents—especially Christian parents.

Knowing that parents watch with sadness and uncertainty as their children struggle to maneuver waves of grief, I became convinced I needed to write this book for you. My dilemma turned me in the direction of a decision. My heart was preparing for what came next.

Why You and I Are Here

The main reason I wrote this book is also the most important thing you need to know about parenting your grieving child. The week after I began, after my quest for resources, I was on a road through the mountains of Central Oregon to Portland. It was a glorious fall day, and my spirit was filled with gratitude. I started to sing, pray, and worship. All the needs of my heart came to the surface. My insecurities, worries, and discomfort were soothed, and the Lord spoke to me: "Amy, one reason I sent my Son, Jesus, to the world was to heal grief. Too many of my children are hurting and grieving. Write this book. Tell them I see them. Tell them I love them. Tell them I will heal them. Tell them Jesus came to bind up their broken hearts."

God always knows what to say.

You and I will walk together on a journey toward healing because God doesn't want his children stuck in grief. That includes you. That includes the beloved child you are worried about. He wants all his children to experience joy and peace through the fullness of relationship with him. Grief and loss are a part of life, but they are not God's ultimate plan for your life. In the Bible, God promises to heal grief and turn mourning into joy (Psalm 30:11; John 16:20). Joy, peace, and abundance are in his plan for you, your child, and the entire world.

"Tell them I see them. Tell them I love them. Tell them I will heal them. Tell them Jesus came to bind up their broken hearts." God always knows what to say.

If you're not a Christian, I believe wholeheartedly that this resource will still be a balm to your wounds, a help to your child, and a guide for your journey. You're going to learn about your child's grief through an integrated perspective of current psychological principles and Christian faith, and you'll learn a lot of parenting skills specific to grieving children.

The Most Important Thing

No matter what road has brought you to this point of need, to your child's ache of loss, the most important thing you need to sustain you is hope. We will gather insights, skills, support, and wisdom for everyday wants and wounds. You will see the real heart of God for you and your child, and you will experience God's warm, comforting healing through his words.

Hope, the most important thing, is where we begin...and God can give us hope in abundance.

1

Provisions for the Journey

Wisdom Principle

Seek wisdom.

If any of you lacks wisdom, you should ask God, who gives generously to all without finding fault, and it will be given to you.

JAMES 1:5

The unthinkable happened. Death. Disaster. Perhaps an accident, illness, or tragedy. A cherished person or an entire family, gone. As a result, your child experienced one of life's tragedies: *great loss*. She's different now. You can see it on her face. You can see it in her body. You can feel it in your heart. She's not the same little girl anymore. This one thing, this great loss, has changed her.

Her heart is broken.

As her parent, your heart breaks too. You want to make it right—to protect her—but you don't know how. This great loss goes beyond what you naturally know to do as a parent. You don't know how to fix this, and you don't know how to fix her.

You both know that things will never, ever be the same again. You are worried and maybe even a little scared. What is the best thing to do? What is the best thing to say? How can you know what she is really feeling and thinking? Is she even grieving the way you think she might be? What if she doesn't get better? What if this great loss sets her on the wrong path and permanently affects her life?

Let me assure you. Your child is going to be okay. She is going to heal, because God sees her. He longs to bind up her broken heart. In fact, binding up the brokenhearted is one of the main assignments of Jesus Christ. Isaiah 61:1-3 is a prophecy of the coming Messiah:

> The Spirit of the Sovereign LORD is on me,
> because the LORD has anointed me
> to preach good news to the poor.
> *He has sent me to bind up the brokenhearted,*
> to proclaim freedom for the captives
> and release from darkness for the prisoners,
> to proclaim the year of the LORD's favor
> and the day of vengeance of our God,
> to comfort all who mourn,
> and provide for those who grieve in Zion—
> to bestow on them a crown of beauty
> instead of ashes,
> the oil of joy
> instead of mourning,
> and a garment of praise
> instead of a spirit of despair.
> They will be called oaks of righteousness,
> a planting of the LORD
> for the display of his splendor.

Jesus is like the nurturing grandma who always knows how to fix it. He's got a great big sewing kit with just the right scissors to cut what needs to be cut, the right needles for tough fabric, and the right thread for the perfect stitches. First stitch: comfort. Second stitch: provision. Third stitch: beauty. Fourth stitch: joy. Quietly, confidently, Jesus is there, mending your child's broken heart stitch after stitch, until finally the fragments of her heart are transformed into a beautiful garment of praise.

Jesus is mending your child's broken heart.

Jesus is going to do another amazing thing. He will turn your child's grief into a source of strength in her life. Look at the last sentence in the quote above: "They will be called oaks of righteousness, a planting of the LORD for the display of his splendor." Imagine the Lord planting a beautiful, strong oak tree by a stream of water. That oak tree provides shade, shelter, and respite. It provides inspiration with its beauty and its majesty. It provides peace.

Your child is that planting of the Lord.

And it doesn't end there. The rest of Isaiah 61 promises that those who grieve will eventually prosper. They will rebuild. They will become ministers and agents of healing. They will receive a double portion. They will rejoice.

Comfort and healing. Strength. Prosperity. A joyful, peaceful life. These are the promises for your child.

So take courage, dear parent. This great loss, while incredibly difficult, is not going to hold your child back. God always fulfills his promises. And one of the ways God is going to fulfill his promises is to use you. Yes, you—even though you probably feel inadequate and overwhelmed because of this huge assignment. The Lord sees you too. He's going to walk this journey with you.

When Grief Hits Home

Many years ago, my family went through a horrible tragedy. We grieved every day. Grief was like a dark cloud that hung over our household, making us feel heavy and stuck. We couldn't move forward. One night, my husband and I watched the popular movie *The Way*, a story about a grieving man who walked the Camino de Santiago, a 600-mile spiritual trek through France and Spain. My husband, a pastor, felt a gentle calling from the Lord: "Get up. Go. Walk. One foot in front of the other. I will walk with you. I will meet you on your journey. My presence will go with you, and I will see the journey to the end." Right there, on the couch in our empty family room, my husband decided to get up and walk.

A 600-mile journey—on foot, no less—takes a bit of planning and preparation. Like the other Camino pilgrims, my husband would carry everything he needed for the 40-day journey on his back. He would need provisions, but he would need just the right provisions because he had a limited capacity to carry the load. Now, don't get me wrong—my husband is a strong man. He can carry a lot. But for this 600-mile journey over high mountains, in harsh and unpredictable conditions, and with no guarantee of food, a bed, or a hot shower, my husband could take only the most important things. He could take only the necessary provisions to see the journey to the end.

It took my husband several months to plan his journey. He read Camino stories written by other pilgrims. He studied weather charts. He wrote packing lists. He purchased the lightest backpacking gear possible. He planned a budget, and he created a contingency plan for emergencies. He wanted to be as prepared as possible.

You should have seen our family room! For months, all his gear, packing lists, and clothing were strewn about. Our living space looked like a tornado had descended on us. But the real tornado that had plowed through our household was our great loss. Knowing that he was going to step forward out of the mess toward healing gave us both a sense of power and purpose.

Gathering What You Need

You and your child are at the beginning of a journey. A journey toward healing. You have a special assignment from the Lord—a calling to parent a grieving child. Parenting is a challenge, even in the best of circumstances. I know that like my husband, you can carry a lot. But grief adds another layer. There are so many unknowns ahead of you, and you cannot take a single step of this journey without being prepared. You need exactly the right provisions to see the journey through to the end. You must carry only what you need to carry. No more and no less.

I imagine you now, thinking about what you need to finish this journey. What should you pack, and what should you leave behind? What do you have now that you can use, and what do you need to acquire? How can you acquire what you need? You will need practical provisions for your day-to-day life. But you also need some essential provisions to keep you walking, especially on the days when you are tired and discouraged. These provisions from God are wisdom and hope.

> You are at the beginning of a journey. A journey toward healing. You have a special assignment from the Lord—a calling to parent a grieving child.

Wisdom is the ability to make good judgments, and it helps us live the best life we can. The Bible says that wisdom comes from God: "The fear [awe, reverence] of the LORD is the beginning of wisdom, and knowledge of the Holy One is understanding" (Proverbs 9:10). Through your relationship with God, he gives you the wisdom you need to live your life in peace. Especially when it comes to parenting your grieving child.

It's going to be very important that you stay close to God through this journey. Seek wisdom from him. As we saw in the verse at the beginning of this chapter, he promises to give it to you if you ask.

One of the best ways any of us can prepare for a journey is to get on our knees. In fact, I encourage you to get on your knees every day and pray. Ask the Holy Spirit to fill you with his presence, and ask the Father to give you wisdom about how to interpret the concepts in this book and how to use them with your child. I know it's hard to believe, but God knows your child better than you do. He loves her more than you do. He knows exactly what she needs to hear and exactly what she needs in order to heal. Ask God for those answers. He will be faithful to provide them for you.

Life will never be the same again because something or someone is missing. Amid the grief, it is hard to see anything good ahead of you. This place of sorrow is dark, cold, and as unpredictable as the journey you are now preparing for. Hope is the expectation that something good will happen at the end of your journey. It is a gift that God gives us for our encouragement, to keep us moving forward. Hope will help you put one foot in front of the other, even when you don't feel like walking anymore. This book will encourage you the whole way, giving you hope when you are exhausted, afraid, or lonely. And during this time that we share and well beyond the turn of the last page, I will be full of hope for you and your child.

Hope is the expectation that something good will happen at the end of your journey. It's a gift that God gives you for your encouragement to keep you moving forward.

Skills for Your Journey

Some years ago, a friend of mine tragically lost her brother in a freak plane accident. My friend's daughter was three at the time of her uncle's death. My friend told me, "I always wondered if his death affected her because she loved her uncle so much. One day he was there, and the next day he was gone. Our entire family was in extreme shock and chaos for a long time. My daughter was so young, I didn't know if she really knew what grief was." The answer is yes. Even if she could not articulate it, the daughter experienced grief, and her life was impacted by the uncle's death. Grief impacts children of all ages. It impacts children who are nonverbal and children who have special needs. Different types of losses also affect the way children experience grief.

My friend was aware of her daughter's grief, but at the time, she didn't know how to put that awareness into action. Her daughter's response to the death was different from the rest of the family's. It's easy to assume children don't experience grief because they don't express it in the same way adults do. But the developmental differences between children and adults lead to big differences in things like physical responses, language, emotions, and behavior. What works to heal or support a grieving adult will rarely be effective with children.

My friend needed to acquire new provisions to help her daughter grieve. She needed to develop skills unique to grief and skills unique to the developmental level of her child. I'll guess it's the same for you. Each chapter of this book highlights a specific skill for parenting your grieving child. These skills are practical, everyday things you can apply. They are based on biblical wisdom and scientific knowledge. The skill for this chapter involves learning about grief through your Christian faith and current science.

PARENTING SKILL

Learn about grief through your Christian faith and psychological principles.

You're on the right path already because this book will teach you about grief, mourning, and healing. You will learn skills that are tailor-made for parenting grieving children, skills based in psychological principles and your Christian faith. Each chapter of this book provides practical suggestions about what you can do right now and activities you can do this week with your child. Also woven throughout this book are Scriptures, prayers, and answers to some of your tough questions. For your convenience, the parenting skills you will learn in this book are listed on pages 197–198. Each skill is paired with a supporting Bible verse. Feel free to copy and post this list where you will see it often. An online version is available at authoramyford.com. Consider memorizing the verses for days when you need extra support. Most important, you will see God's heartfelt love for grieving children. You will know that Jesus is the Healer and that he longs to mend your child's broken heart.

My husband stepped out in faith and walked the healing journey to which God called him. Every step of the way, God mended my husband's broken heart. God also healed our family. And now, God is beckoning you and your child on your own journey toward healing. God isn't going to simply sit back and watch you go. No, he's right beside you and your child, walking with you. He's your friend and partner on this journey. He's smiling at you, saying, "You're going to make it." He, too, brought an essential provision: the needle and thread from his great big sewing kit. Just like that nurturing grandma, he's going to mend. He's going to heal your broken hearts, every step of the way.

Jesus,

I have a long journey ahead of me, and [your child's name] does too. I'm not even sure how to prepare or where to begin. I ask you to walk this journey with us. We can't do it alone. You have promised in Isaiah 61:1-3 that you will heal and bless my child through this great loss. Help us move toward your healing and blessing. I believe that something good awaits at the end of our journey. I place my hope in you, and I trust that we will experience your presence every step of the way.

Amen.

Q: What is the oil of gladness?

A: The oil of gladness is not a metaphor; it is a real thing. In ancient Jewish culture, the oil of gladness was a special essential oil—a blend of myrrh, cinnamon, calamus, cassia, and olive oil (Exodus 30:22-30). It is called the oil of gladness because when God's people applied it in faith and obedience, God restored their joy. It was used specifically to anoint people and things—to recognize a special calling by God and to be set apart for his service.

When we present ourselves to the Lord to be anointed, the Holy Spirit fills and empowers us. When we are walking in our anointing, we experience the fullness of joy. Isaiah 61:3 assures us that the Messiah will give this oil of gladness to those who mourn. This promise means that Jesus will replace your child's mourning with joy and set her apart to walk according to her special calling.

Steps Toward Healing

Draw Strength from This Chapter

- One of Jesus's main assignments is to heal grief.
- Your grieving child is promised comfort, healing, strength, prosperity, and a joyful, peaceful life.
- Parents of grieving children need essential provisions for the journey: wisdom, hope, and skills unique to caring for grieving children.

What You Can Do Right Now

- Pray the chapter prayer over your child.
- Meditate on God's promises for your child (Isaiah 61:1-3).
- Meditate on James 1:5. Ask the Lord for wisdom. Write down what the Holy Spirit is prompting you to do to gain wisdom. Reflect on what you've done well to help your child grieve, as well as what you might need to do differently. What can you celebrate? What do you need to learn? Jot down a few notes.
- Create a reading schedule to finish this book. (Yes, put it on your daily planner!)
- Identify supportive people in your child's life. Share this book with them and ask them to read it so that they can support you and your child.

Activities You Can Do This Week with Your Child

- Read Isaiah 61:1-3 and Exodus 30:22-30 to your child. You may need to find a simple Bible translation or explain what these passages mean to your child in language she understands.

- If financially feasible, purchase an essential oil that smells like joy to you. Check Etsy, Walmart, or Christian-based essential oil companies. (You can find the oil of gladness blend already made, or you can find another blend. Any oil will do because oil represents the presence of the Holy Spirit.) Diffuse the oil in your child's bedroom and throughout your home. If she asks, tell your child that you want to make the house smell joyful.
- Search the Bible for a verse about hope. Ask your child to draw a picture about something hopeful. When she's finished, write the verse you found on the bottom of her picture. Put the picture in a place where everyone can see it (like the refrigerator) as a reminder that God is mending things.

Art by Emmalle, age 10

2

When You're Grieving Too

Wisdom Principle

Your child's job is to grieve. Your job is to be the parent as he grieves.

[Parents], do not embitter your children, or they will become discouraged.

Colossians 3:21

Life might be very hard right now. Responsibilities are popping up faster than Playskool Busy Poppin' Pals, and you just can't seem to keep them all down. You're dealing with your own life while parenting a child who suddenly has very distinct needs. Plus, you have to make dinner, clean the cat fur off the couch, do three loads of laundry, and write those work emails you left unfinished because you had to pick up your kid early from a canceled karate practice.

Chances are, you're completely exhausted. And there might be a darker layer underneath all of it too—your own grief. Perhaps you experienced the great loss right along with your child. Or perhaps you look at what happened to him, and your heart begins to distrust goodness and beauty in the world. These feelings are so very painful, and they make you feel lonely because no one else seems to get it.

When you experience loneliness day after day, night after night, you begin to feel really discouraged. It's hard to find hope on the dark days. It's even harder to find a friend. God wired us for human connection and relationship, and we need them the most during tough times. As adults, we know this principle rationally. But sometimes our discouragement clouds our judgment, and we reach out to whatever seems to immediately take the pain away. Sometimes unhealthy things, like too much food or alcohol. Staying in bed all day. Refusing to take care of the bills, or indulgence in things that will only bring us more trouble.

It's hard to take care of anyone else—even your own child—when your needs are so great. The verse that provides the foundation for this chapter's wisdom principle, Colossians 3:21, uses the word "embitter," which means to cause someone to feel resentful. People feel resentment when their needs are chronically unmet. You might be feeling that resentment right now because no one is meeting your needs.

Children are no different. When their needs go unmet, they, too, can carry resentment day after day, night after night. Eventually they also become deeply discouraged. And amid this great loss, that understanding is perhaps the most difficult for you. You know your child has important needs, but you aren't sure you can provide for him.

Overwhelmed. So much to do. Feeling sad and so inadequate. Let me encourage you. This chapter provides some simple ideas about how you can take care of your child while taking care of yourself.

Attunement

You have a big task list. Take care of this child—check. Provide for all his needs so he can grow up to be a productive, healthy adult—check. Meet his extra emotional needs while he is grieving—um...check? Deep inside, you know that attending to your child's emotional needs is the biggest priority. The psychological word for attending to a child's emotional needs is "attunement." Children learn closeness, bonding, and intimacy very early in life from their caregivers, which is known as "attachment." Research shows that securely attached children can form other emotionally healthy relationships as they grow, which leads to success throughout life. When you attune positively to your child, you help him form healthy, secure attachments.

Attuned parenting is a wise parenting principle. We see in Colossians 3:21 that God's intention was for parents to be attuned to their children. Parents must meet their children's needs so they can develop properly. When children's emotional needs are met consistently, they live lives of hope and encouragement rather than lives of despair.

Don't worry about being a perfect parent. Your child most values relationship and connection with you.

So what does attuned parenting look like? Does it mean you must meet all your child's wishes or demands? Of course not. Attuned parenting simply means being aware of your child's emotional needs and responding to his emotions as affirmatively and quickly as possible. Attunement does not mean you can't discipline your child when he misbehaves. Nor does it mean you must give in to his every wish. It's simply recognizing and validating your child's feelings first—before providing structure or correction.

For example, Marcos, a grieving six-year-old boy, doesn't want to sleep in his own room. He wants to sleep with his parent instead. He seems anxious and afraid at night. This behavior is different from his behavior before the loss. It results in a power struggle every night, and the parent is tempted to give in just to avoid a fight. However, the parent knows this behavior cannot continue as Marcos grows. Here is an example of an attuned response:

> Marcos, I wonder if you're feeling scared of sleeping in your bed tonight. I'm here, and there's nothing to be afraid of. I'm going to read you a story, and then I'll turn off your light. I'll sit here for 15 minutes before I leave. You will sleep in your bed tonight, and I'll sleep in mine.

Marcos's attuned parent immediately recognizes and validates his feelings but also sets a boundary. The parent should then follow through with the boundary and continue to do so as needed. The parent didn't get angry, and the parent refused to fight. The parent's boundary was set on principle for Marcos's best interests in the long run.

Attunement is the biggest check mark on that parenting task list.

If all you can do right now is attune to your child's emotions, that's enough. If you need some help with your child's physical needs or with your personal needs, then get help. Be willing to let go of your idea of a perfect parent. The house can be messy for a while. Obviously, your child does need adequate food, clothing, shelter, and rest, but when it comes to the extras that parents want to give their kids, children are generally forgiving, and they do just fine if you don't manage the house perfectly. Your child most values his relationship and connection with you, and your attending to his feelings in return.

The Parent Is the Parent, and the Child Is the Child

God gave us an amazing ability to experience feelings and to understand the feelings of other people. This ability is called empathy, and it's a necessity for human relationship. People begin to develop empathy and recognize emotion within a month or two after birth. This is why babies are so fascinated with people's faces and begin to make their own facial expressions and sounds in response. It's like fine-tuned emotional radar.

This emotional radar helps children in a few ways. First, it helps them develop relationships with others. They learn to sense other people's emotional states and to respond appropriately. Healthy children usually express curiosity, love, compassion, or concern for other people. Second, the emotional radar helps children sense whether they are safe by gauging the emotions of their caretakers. If their caretakers appear relaxed, stable, and secure, the child will feel the same. But if their caretakers are anxious, overwhelmed, or angry, children also will feel the same.

Children develop and manage their feelings through their emotional radar until early adolescence. At that stage, they begin to individuate from their caregivers. They learn to distinguish their own feelings and communicate them. But if your child is younger, he not only picks up on your emotions but also adapts them as his own. Younger children will assimilate more of your emotions; older children will probably assimilate less, but they are still receptive of your emotional state.

Your child loves you very much and is naturally inclined toward compassion and empathy for you. This quality is wonderful, but it also presents a danger: Your child may attempt to become your caretaker. This is most likely to happen with children who are sensitive to emotion, children with capable and strong personalities, and children who grow up with impaired parents. The term for this is "parentification," which is a role reversal of the parent and child. The child becomes the parent, and the parent displays dependent behavior on the child.

Let's pause for a moment. Since you are reading this book, I know you're concerned about being a good parent. I know you are doing your very best to be attuned to your child's needs, and I am confident you are succeeding. But great loss drastically changes things, and the good skills you would use under normal circumstances might be a challenge right now.

Your child also is very aware of your emotional state. He's experiencing it too. There is a possibility that he might try to become the caretaker when he sees problems. For him, it might be the only way to gain mastery over his situation.

How do children caretake? They stay very attuned to *your* feelings. They might try to be your main source of comfort or protection. They may try to take on responsibility for which they are not developmentally ready, such as "being the man of the house" or cooking dinner for the family. Older siblings might take care of younger siblings—feeding and washing them, getting them off to school, and enforcing a bedtime. Parentification happens when children do, say, or feel anything in the parent's place. These things usually are not within the child's developmental abilities, and a child should not be responsible for them.

Great loss drastically changes things, and the good skills you would use under normal circumstances might be a challenge right now.

When your heart is broken, it's easy to let your child soothe your pain. After all, he loves you so much, and you love him. You share a bond that will never be ruptured. He's right there, all the time. He experienced the same thing you did. You're family. He gets it. It's almost as if you mistake your child for your friend.

But here's a tough question: If you are your child's friend, who is his parent?

The parent-child relationship is not equal, and God never designed it to be. Your job as a parent is to provide for your child's needs, including his need for correction and discipline. This role means there is always a power dynamic. Authority and mutuality cannot coexist. When one person has authority over another, real mutuality between them is impossible. God created the parent-child relationship to be unequal so that children's needs can be met and they can grow into healthy, productive adults who meet the needs of their own children, spouses, workplaces, and communities. This maturity happens when the child's needs are met by a caring adult with no expectation for him to meet any of the adult's needs.

If children are expected or allowed to take a mutual emotional role with an adult who should be taking care of their emotional needs, they can quickly become resentful because their emotional needs go unmet. But this dynamic is hidden—your child won't express that resentment to you (now) because of the parent-child power dynamic. Nor does he have the brain capability to be aware of that resentment and talk about it.

Your child's only job right now is to process his grief and to move forward in a healthy way. He is not developmentally capable of taking care of all his emotional needs, so he couldn't possibly meet yours. He needs a parent who can meet his needs with no expectation of reciprocity. We've arrived at our second parenting skill, which is to take care of your child and not allow your child to be your caretaker.

PARENTING SKILL

Take care of your child, and do not allow your child to be your caretaker.

Caring for Yourself *Is* Caring for Your Child

Now let's get to the encouraging part. I'm glad you've hung in there with me through this chapter. It's been a tough one because you are grieving too.

You are just as important as your child. Your needs are legitimate, and you deserve to have your needs met. You do need a friend, or friends, who get it. You need a strong support system to get you through this season. You might even need financial support, day care, or assistance with maintenance around the house. Seek out this help. Find some wise, caring people you can talk to, such as healthy family members, friends, a support group, or your pastor. See a professional counselor if you need one. Make sure you do things you love. Get out for dinner with your friends. Go hunting. Get a massage. Keep up with your hobbies. Visit people who love and support you. Make moderate exercise and eating nutritious food high priorities. Do it all freely with no guilt, no explanation, and no apologies.

If you're struggling with unhealthy habits or addiction, it's time to get some help. Find a local recovery resource, such as Celebrate Recovery or Alcoholics Anonymous / Narcotics Anonymous. These resources are free, and they will provide the support and accountability you need.

If you can't do these things for your own sake, do them for your child. When you are healthy, you dramatically increase the likelihood that your child will be healthy. Remember, his emotional radar is assimilating your feelings all the time. If he sees you taking care of yourself, he'll take care of himself. He'll have the emotional permission to move forward in a healthy way without you ever saying a word. It's one of the biggest paradoxes ever. Taking care of yourself is one of the best ways you can take care of your child.

I know it's not easy. You're grieving. You endure long, lonely nights and spontaneous tearful episodes. Perhaps you've even had a few 0-to-60 emotional meltdowns. Taking care of yourself does not mean hiding your feelings. Let your child see you grieve—and then let him see you take care of your grief in a healthy way. Healthy emotional living includes fully feeling your feelings, even when they leak out all over the place. It means accepting your feelings as legitimate and giving yourself permission to feel them.

But healthy emotional living also includes being responsible for your feelings. You take care of them with developmentally appropriate people and measures. You apologize if you lose it. You don't allow your child to carry your feelings, resolve them, or be your main source of comfort.

Taking care of yourself is one of the best ways you can take care of your child.

It's setting basic boundaries with your child, which you do all the time as a parent. Be attuned to yourself while you are attuned to your child. Don't allow your child to attune to you and become your caretaker. Let your child see you take care of yourself and your emotions in a healthy way, and I guarantee he will be on the right path to an emotionally healthy life himself. When you are meeting your own needs and practicing your own self-care, you are naturally attuning. And you create trust within your child's heart. He trusts that his needs will be met consistently—especially his need to grieve.

Jesus,

You have given me this child as a blessing, and I want to meet my child's needs. Sometimes I feel so overwhelmed about how to parent, especially now. I'm dealing with my own grief. I choose to press into you and trust you for my own healing. Please move toward me, Holy Spirit, and give me the wisdom to know how to best attune to my child's needs. Please manifest yourself in my heart and in my home so I can keep my eyes on you and not on my pain. Thank you, Jesus, for seeing my pain and for promising to heal us both. I feel your presence and your comfort.

Amen.

Q: What if I missed attunement?

A: What happens if you've missed attunement, or you've failed to set good emotional boundaries, or you haven't modeled healthy emotional responses? Don't worry. You can correct from here. You can start today by using the skills in this book. Younger children will likely respond to this change very positively. You will see improved behavior and a reduction in their emotional meltdowns as well as more loving responses to you.

If you have an older child or teen who seems to be taking on the role of the parent, say something like this:

> It's been hard on all of us for a long time. I haven't been the best parent I can be. God is teaching me what I need to do to take care of myself so I can take care of you. I want you to know that I really, really appreciate all you've been doing to help me and our family. But you're not the parent. I am. You get to be the kid, and I get to meet your needs. From now on, I'll make all the parent decisions, and I will take care of you. I might ask you to help me sometimes, but I will still make the decisions. I love you very much. We're going to get through this. I'm so glad you're my [son/daughter].

This kind of communication with a child who has begun taking on the role of the parent might provoke some anxiety, and you might experience a power struggle because he's used to being in control. Be consistent and firm, and eventually he will respect the boundary you have set.

Steps Toward Healing

Draw Strength from This Chapter

- Attuning to your child requires consistently attending to his emotional needs.
- Setting boundaries with your child will help meet his long-term emotional needs.
- Practicing good self-care is one of the best ways to take care of your child.

What You Can Do Right Now

- Pray the chapter prayer over your child.
- Meditate on Colossians 3:21. Ask God to show you what you can do to encourage your child. Ask God to show you boundaries you might need to set with your child. Jot down a few notes.
- Reflect on how you've practiced your own self-care. What has gone well? What do you need to improve? Write down two things you will do in the next week to practice your own self-care. Put those things on your day planner.

Activities You Can Do This Week with Your Child

- Have your child draw a picture of things he loves or enjoys. Ask him to tell you about each thing, and then affirm his feelings: "You love the color blue." "You love pizza." This affirmation helps your child become aware of his own individual feelings. It also shows him you are attuned to his feelings.
- Find an activity you both enjoy. For you, practice self-care. For your child, give him an opportunity to connect with

you. For example, go jogging and have your child follow on his bike.

- With younger children, practice attuned play for 15 minutes. Let your child direct all the activities, and respond to his communication and feelings in a positive way. During this time, do not correct your child. Let those 15 minutes be all about him. This time is not about teaching or correcting your child; rather, it's for affirming your child. This affirmation lets him know that he is acceptable and valuable, which builds positive self-esteem.

Don't worry about being a perfect parent. Take good care of yourself so you can take care of me.

Art by Cynthia, age 9

3

Rest, Breathe, Connect

Wisdom Principle

Taking care of your grieving child's body and brain is just as important as taking care of her heart.

I praise you because I am fearfully and wonderfully made; your works are wonderful, I know that full well.

Psalm 139:14

Do you remember the first time you laid eyes on your child? That moment may have been filled with intensity and pain, but I'll guess it also was filled with absolute awe. This little human with whom you were entrusted was *yours*, and she was absolutely...perfect. All her fingers and toes, her beautiful eyes, and her perfect chin dimple. In that moment, you sensed the meaning of King David's words: "I am fearfully and wonderfully made."

The human body is an absolute masterpiece, created by the Master Artist. Grieving children have broken hearts. But what about broken bodies? We don't always think about the body, but grief impacts the body and brain just as much as it does the heart. And this impact has some big implications for your child's behavior.

A Perfect Piece of Machinery

Your child's body is like a car. It has an outer frame that keeps everything together and inner workings that make her go. If all the mechanics are working properly, your child runs well. If something is out of order, your child doesn't get very far—and neither do you!

One of the most amazing parts of the human body is the brain. An easy way to understand the brain's role in the body is to think of it as the driver of the body-car. It manages everything your child does, says, thinks, and feels. The brain has three parts: the brain stem, the cerebellum, and the cerebrum. The brain stem and cerebellum coordinate automatic and basic survival functions (such as breath and heartbeat) and motor activity (movement). The cerebrum, the largest part of the brain, coordinates higher functions, such as thinking and emotion.

These three parts exist simultaneously but develop at different paces. The survival brain begins developing at conception, and its purpose is to help the baby survive in the womb and after birth. The emotional brain begins developing in full force one or two months after birth. You probably remember the first time your baby smiled at you. That smile was a sign that her emotional brain was developing. The thinking brain starts developing more rapidly around puberty, but it is not fully developed until adulthood. This is why children and teens make decisions based on emotion instead of logic. They need help with executive functioning (including planning, reasoning, and recognizing cause and effect) and skills mastery for self-sufficiency until they become adults.

Survival Brain	**(brain stem and cerebellum)**	manages physical survival, such as breathing, digestion, sleep, motor activity, posture, balance, and reproduction
Emotional Brain	**(cerebrum)**	manages emotion, attachment, bonding, fear response, and emotional memory
Thinking Brain		manages reason, logic, abstraction, planning, problem solving, memory, and language

To better understand the brain's structure, let's think about it in relation to my friend who was unsure whether her three-year-old daughter was grieving the death of her uncle. The daughter was indeed grieving, but because of her brain's developmental stage, she could not express grief like the rest of the family. Her ability to identify her own feelings and express them verbally had not developed yet. Her emotional radar picked up on the family's emotional responses, and she began expressing that same intensity through her behavior—clinging, tantrums, and disobedience.

The brain's development has some big implications for parenting a grieving child. Since your child's survival brain and emotional brain develop faster than her thinking brain, she will process her grief primarily with her survival and emotional brains and then express that grief through behavior and emotion rather than through reason and language. The younger your child is, the more this will be true. Children who have reached adolescence may be better able to process grief through reason and language.

The Gas Pedal

Processing a stressor, such as grief or loss, is like stepping down hard on the gas pedal in the brain-body car. Stress impacts the human body through the autonomic nervous system, which sends signals to the muscles and organs (including the brain) when faced with a stressor. Have you heard of "fight, flight, or freeze"? When faced with a stressor, people instinctively respond by fighting the stressor, running from it, or shutting down. These responses from the nervous system are automatic. Everybody—including your child—responds to stress behaviorally and emotionally with little or no thought involved.

The fight, flight, or freeze mechanism is often helpful because it keeps us safe from legitimate threats. Fight, flight, or freeze is the mechanism children use to process grief. These are some of ways your child might respond as her nervous system revs up:

Fight (Looks like Aggression)

having an angry or mean facial expression

showing anger

being irritable

acting out

misbehaving

having temper tantrums

having meltdowns

bothering others

exhibiting behavior problems at school

showing physical aggression (kicking, hitting, biting, spitting)

being impulsive

talking back to adults

showing a decline in school performance (because of behavior problems)

Flight (Looks like Anxiety)

having an anxious or fearful facial expression

hiding

disappearing

wanting to leave

asking constant, worried questions

showing anxiety

having nightmares and sleep problems

having somatic problems

having tummy aches and bathroom problems

clinging to adults

being impulsive

overeating, sneaking food, or being concerned with food

exhibiting immature behaviors

showing a decline in school performance (because of difficulty concentrating)

Freeze (Looks like Depression)

having a numb or dazed facial expression

shutting down emotionally

staying in room or refusing to be around others

denying or unable to express feelings

not responding to contact with others

not showing interest in food or play

not showing interest in love, hugs, or touch

taking too long to complete tasks

exhibiting aggression to self, such as self-harm

showing a decline in school performance (because of disinterest or not caring)

These behaviors might not make sense to you. After all, doesn't your child know that misbehaving will cause her more stress in the end? The answer is no, she does not understand this yet. She does not think, "*If* I kick my brother, *then* I will get into trouble, which will cause me more problems today and make me feel worse than I do right now." Her thinking brain has not developed enough to reason through cause and effect.

Instead, the emotional brain manages her stress response. A stressor (the loss) appears. Her survival brain sends a message to her body: *Danger, survive!* Her body then reacts (fight, flight, or freeze) in defense. Her feeling brain reacts at the same time: *Danger, fear!* Her endocrine system pumps a flood of stress hormones to give her the extra burst of energy to deal with the stressor.

And that's what happens—disorganized behavior or emotions. There is no cause and effect, reason, or even language in your child's grief.

To complicate things, grief is not a onetime or short-lived stressor. Grief stays around awhile. Perhaps your family is having severe and ongoing emotional responses to the great loss. Perhaps your child had a major transition because of the loss, like moving to a new home or going to a new school. Perhaps there are new financial difficulties, which result in a change of lifestyle. These secondary adjustments become stressors of their own. And because your child's brain has not resolved the first stressor (the great loss), her brain will define these new adjustments as stressors as well. These unresolved stressors pile up, and your child begins to show a pattern of fight, flight, or freeze.

Now your child's responses are starting to make sense. She's not misbehaving on purpose. Her brain and her body are responding automatically. She's simply trying to process her grief in the only way she is developmentally capable of right now. Your child cannot process grief through her thinking brain if it is not fully developed. She's processing her grief through the survival brain (her physical body) and the emotional brain (her instinct to fight, flight, or freeze). The best thing you can do to help her release that grief is to practice our third parenting skill, which is to take extra good care of your child's physical body.

PARENTING SKILL

Take extra good care of your child's physical body.

The Brakes

God created our autonomic (sympathetic) nervous system to rev up in the face of stress, but he also created a mechanism for slowing it down. Another part of the nervous system, the parasympathetic nervous system, is often referred to as "the brakes." This system is activated by a few very simple things: rest, breath, and human connection.

Stress Response (sympathetic nervous system)	Stress Recovery (parasympathetic nervous system)
fight, flight, freeze	rest, breathe, connect

We are fearfully and wonderfully made. God gave us a mechanism to respond to stress, and he gave us a mechanism to recover from stress. Taking care of your child's physical body simply means activating her stress recovery response system in three simple ways:

1. Increasing rest and creating more opportunities for rest.
2. Encouraging your child to slow down and breathe and creating more opportunities for deep breath.
3. Increasing your child's relational connection with you and other supportive people.

Rest is simply slowing down—taking more quiet time, sleeping more, making weekends restful, and taking vacations. These actions repair the damage stress has caused in the muscles, joints, and organs. Breath, particularly deep breath, slows down the heart rate and fills the body with fresh oxygen, helping the body eliminate toxins. Human connection opens the heart to feeling safe again. Skin-to-skin contact increases oxytocin, a chemical important for human bonding. The need for connection is a good reason to give extra hugs and snuggles to your child and to engage in play with her. Here are a few ideas to increase rest, breath, and connection in your home:

Rest (Emphasizing Relaxation in Your Home)

Practice a Sabbath day once a week.

Cook and serve foods that are nonstimulating.

Keep noise low.

Keep high-energy people away for a while.

Keep activity at a minimum.

Keep to a simple but consistent schedule.

Take a low-key family trip to the beach or mountains.

Get your child on a consistent sleep schedule with extra rest time.

Make sure her sleeping space is a place where she enjoys spending time.

Breath (Emphasizing Peace in Your Home)

Implement regular but gentle exercise.

Go to the park or pool regularly.

Go hunting for frogs or rocks, or go for family bicycle rides.

Teach your child to calm herself and "deep breathe" when she is feeling stressed.

Try relaxing exercises, such as stretching or hiking.

Get outside.

Garden.

Find a farm and visit animals.

Connection (Emphasizing Love and Hope in Your Home)

Offer more hugs and snuggles.

Establish a regular family night with movies, games, or other low-energy activities.

Eat together.

Cook fun and new foods together.

Read books out loud.

Make lots of eye contact.

Attend activities with supportive people.

Get a new pet.

If your child refuses to participate, gently keep asking.

Say "I love you" and "You're important to me."

I'm sure you are already emphasizing rest, breath, and connection because they are parts of a healthy family life. But grieving children need these in extra large doses. Make them intentional practices every day. If your child has special needs and cannot respond verbally, remember that she is experiencing stress and will require your help in activating her stress recovery response. You are probably aware of the ways your child expresses stress. Watch for those signs and then introduce rest, breath, and connection to your child in ways that work for her.

If you're having a hard time doing this on a regular basis, elicit help from supportive people. Perhaps your child's uncle or her friend's parent would be happy to plan some special time with your child, which could give you a break to practice some self-care. (Rest, breath, and connection are important for you too!)

Every long journey requires rest breaks. It might feel counterintuitive to make these breaks a priority, especially when you know you have a long journey ahead. However, rest brings just as much healing as does forward movement. Your body and brain need downtime to repair and renew. If you don't rest, finishing the journey will be impossible. Rest is a tool God gave us to help us get through stressful and difficult situations. Take some time right now to slow down and rest. Breathe. Spend some time connecting with God, meditating on his Word and his promises for you and your child.

Rest brings just as much healing as does forward movement.

God,

We are made in your image, and we are fearfully and wonderfully made. I am eager to learn how I can best respond to my child's physical needs during this great loss. I welcome your teaching and wisdom, even scientific concepts about our wonderful bodies that you created. Help me use the skills I learned in this chapter to help my child rest, breathe, and connect. I know that you are here, Jesus. I envision you beside us, helping us connect not only with each other but also with you.

Amen.

Q: What is a Sabbath day?

A: A Sabbath day is an intentional day of rest once per week that the Lord asks his people to observe (Genesis 2:2-3; Exodus 20:8-11). It is a way to worship, honor, and connect with God, who restores our energy through Sabbath practice. Throughout Scripture, God emphasized the need for a Sabbath (Psalm 118:24; Hebrews 4:9) and showed frustration when it was not observed (Ezekiel 20:13; 22:8).

God designed our bodies to rest. Many Christian denominations recognize the Sabbath as the day they attend church, and Sabbath traditions vary. However, in busy American culture, we can lose sight of this intentional practice. We can observe Sabbath in various ways: Avoid all work, intentionally rest (nap or do something fun), spend time with loved ones, eat a meal out, or have a special dessert. Some people may follow a more traditional approach and turn off technology, avoid doing business or cooking food, or other significant measures to preserve the day for only rest. Pray and ask God to show you how to observe a Sabbath day in your home.

Rest helps us heal.

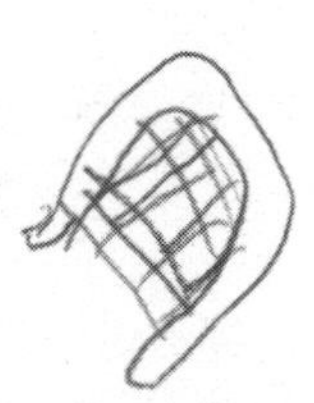

Art by Cynthia, age 9

Steps Toward Healing

Draw Strength from This Chapter

- Children, because of their stage of brain development, process grief primarily through behavior and emotion rather than reason and language.
- People automatically respond to stress through fight, flight, or freeze.
- You can take care of your child's brain and body by providing extra rest, breath, and connection.

What You Can Do Right Now

- Pray the chapter prayer over your child.
- Meditate on Psalm 139:14. Give thanks for how awesome the Lord has made your child. Ask the Lord to help you understand how to care for your child's physical needs.
- Reflect on your child's behavior since the great loss. What stress response does she seem to show the most—fight, flight, or freeze? Jot some notes about how you might be able to recognize triggers in the future.

Activities You Can Do This Week with Your Child

- Take a Sabbath day with your child and family. Talk about what Sabbath is and why it's important. Read Psalm 118:24, Mark 2:27, or Hebrews 4:9 to your child. Involve your child in creating a family Sabbath.
- Schedule some individual special time with your child. What nonstimulating activity does she love to do? It doesn't have to be expensive, just low stress, fun, and

relational. Focus on rest, breath, and connection. Have a special time weekly if possible.

- Work with your child to make a personal rest space. This space is usually her bedroom, but it can be another area of your home. If your budget allows, redecorate or find some special ways to make her personal space a nonstimulating place she enjoys.

4

Speaking the Unspeakable

Wisdom Principle

Speak the truth with love and hope.

Speaking the truth in love, we will grow to become in every respect the mature body of him who is the head, that is, Christ.

Ephesians 4:15

It's been a year since Mary's husband was killed in a hunting accident. Mary and her three kids have gotten through the initial shock and the memorial service, and they're learning to navigate the day-to-day without their beloved daddy. On lonely nights, Mary flashes back to the night her husband died. She'll never forget the police officer standing on her front porch. And she'll never forget how she collapsed into a heap on the floor, only to glance to the top of the stairs to see her oldest daughter standing there, watching the whole scene.

They've managed. But Mary wonders how her kids are really doing. It's hard for her to talk about their dad's death. She doesn't know what to say or how to say it—or if she should say anything at all. Her kids don't bring it up, especially her middle child, who was diagnosed on the autism spectrum several years ago. But something deep inside tells Mary they all need to talk about it—together.

Mary tries to imagine sitting down with her nine-year-old daughter and seven-year-old and three-year-old sons. Her daughter has been withdrawn this past year and says, "I don't want to talk about Daddy" when the subject comes up. Her middle child seems unaware and uninterested, and his needs haven't changed at all. He rarely speaks anyway, and when he does, he usually gestures or grunts. Mary isn't sure her youngest understands death or even remembers his father. He was only two when his father died.

Children Say the Strangest Things!

Even more challenging, Mary is still reeling from the other day when she and her two youngest were watching her daughter's soccer game. Her three-year-old suddenly announced to the stranger sitting next to them, "My daddy is dead. He got shot, and he had blood all over his face."

Awkward moment...and a painful one too. Grieving children might drop big communication bombs. This behavior is completely normal because they are simply trying to process their grief, not to embarrass you or misbehave. If you can keep this principle in mind, it's easier to know how to handle an awkward situation: Attune to your child's grief, but gently educate him about the best time and way to express it. Mary could gently and quietly address her child first and then say, "You are really trying to work out in your mind what happened to Daddy. It's important to you to talk about it. But let's talk about it later because this nice person didn't know Daddy."

After giving her child a hug, Mary could then turn to the stranger and say, "Thank you for listening," and move on. This simple statement acknowledges the stranger's potential discomfort without invalidating her child's feelings. She doesn't need to apologize for her child, and she doesn't need to explain the great loss.

Some Normal Ways Children Talk About Their Losses

- asking curious questions, such as "Did it hurt Daddy when he died?" or "Will it hurt when I die?"
- asking difficult questions or making awkward statements, sometimes completely out of the blue, especially to strangers or people outside of your family

- drawing pictures of the deceased, including pictures of the death of the deceased
- drawing pictures of the funeral, the burial, or any other death rituals
- playacting the deceased, the death, the funeral, or the surviving parent or family
- going silent, whether by going completely mute or speaking only with selected people, toys, or pets
- lying about the death or whereabouts of the deceased or embellishing the details of the death

Your Child's Language Ability

Mary is aware of biblical wisdom about speaking the truth in love. For her, it would mean being able to have an honest conversation with her kids. She wants them to know that she understands their feelings and that it's okay for them to talk about their daddy. She wants them to know how proud of them their daddy would be. But how do you speak about the unspeakable, especially with children? For Mary, it's a task times three—three children at different ages with different needs and different levels of understanding.

In chapter 3, we explored a little bit about your child's brain. Language (verbal communication) is managed by the brain. Children with normal development have two primary language abilities: preverbal and verbal. Older children and teens demonstrate increasing abstraction, which is the ability to infer deeper meanings from communication. Children with developmental abnormalities sometimes have difficulty developing language. They can be nonverbal, which means they communicate without words.

Preverbal

Your child has not yet fully developed the ability to understand you or speak to you. Normally, 100 percent of a child's communication is understandable by age four.

Verbal

Your child can understand you and speak to you. His communication is concrete (literal). His ability to infer deeper meaning in communication (abstraction) increases with age. Children ages eight to eleven have greater abstraction, whereas children ages three to seven have less. Teens have increasing abstraction and usually can communicate like adults.

Nonverbal

Your child is four or older, but he has not fully developed the ability to understand you or speak to you. He may not communicate with words at all. This often indicates the presence of a developmental or speech/language disability.

Each of Mary's children is at his or her own developmental stage and language ability. She has a verbal child who is quickly advancing toward abstract thought. She has a child who is mostly nonverbal, and she has a child who is transitioning from preverbal to concrete verbal. Mary will need to adapt her communication approach for each of her children. Here some principles parents can use.

Preverbal and Nonverbal Children

Talk with your child about the death or loss. Use simple language and short statements, sharing only basic concepts. Ask your child questions to find out how much he understands. Use alternative methods of communication if your child understands them, such as sign language, writing, or pictures. Recognize that preverbal and nonverbal children may not respond to you, and they may not show any emotional change. Emphasize to your child that his response is acceptable, whatever it may be.

Verbal

Talk with your child about the death or loss. Use the same kinds of words he uses so he will understand you. That will mean using concrete language with younger children but speaking to teens the way you would speak to an adult. Use questions to reveal your child's understanding of the communication. Be ready for questions, including some unusual questions. Emphasize to your child that his response is acceptable, whatever it may be.

Speaking Your Child's Language

Once when I was traveling in Italy, two young Japanese tourists approached me. They were lost and needed directions. I was delighted to try to help them, but within seconds, we realized I wouldn't be able to. They spoke Japanese and I spoke English, and to complicate things, we were doing our best to communicate in the very little Italian we knew. The scene on that street corner was probably comical as we gestured and pointed, shaking our heads and saying, "*Ripetere, ripetere*" (Repeat, repeat)! We simply could not communicate no matter how hard we tried. We didn't speak each other's language.

Talking with your children often feels like that. You try to get your message across, but your child speaks another language. Despite this language disconnection, you must find a way to communicate with your child about the great loss. Mary's intuition that her children need to talk about their loss is spot-on. Understanding each one of her children's language abilities helps her know *how* to communicate, but she needs a structure to know *what* to say. We have arrived at our fourth parenting skill, which is to communicate about the great loss honestly and with hope.

PARENTING SKILL

Communicate about the great loss honestly and with hope.

The structure for doing so includes four simple principles that help Mary shape her conversations with her children:

Be honest.

Acknowledge that death or loss means permanent change.

Attune to your child's feelings.

Encourage and educate with hopeful language.

Be Honest

Parents often wonder if they should be honest about death or loss, especially if the death was traumatic. Honesty is essential. Your child is going to hear about it from others, but you should be the one to give him correct information and share your values about death and loss. Giving your child an opportunity to process the loss out loud is important. Children don't often initiate difficult conversations. Talking about the loss gives your child permission to process his feelings out loud.

Younger children are concrete thinkers, which means that they take information literally. They don't yet have the capacity to infer deeper meanings in communication. They need to hear very clearly what the death or loss is and what it means. Sometimes parents are afraid of the impact such honesty will have on their children, so they try to soften their language. For example, children are often told, "Your daddy is with Jesus now." Concrete thinkers may not completely understand this statement; they may think that their dad moved away or went to church. Use specific words, such as "died" or "death," rather than abstract phrases, such as "passed away" or "went to heaven." Coach adults who interact with your children to refer to death as death.

Parents sometimes fear that too many details will traumatize their children—and for good reason. Children need honesty, but they need only simple details. They need to understand what happened in case they overhear others talking about the great loss. They need answers to their questions. Younger children need fewer details, but older children may be more curious and want more details. You will know how many details your child needs by the questions he asks you. Start by explaining the basic details and then answer your child's questions as simply as possible.

Acknowledge the Permanent Change

Many children, especially younger children, don't understand the permanency of death or loss. When parents don't explain that death is permanent, they can misunderstand their children's grief responses. When children don't understand the permanency of loss, they may not grieve until they are fully impacted by the change the loss brought about. Their grief might come long after the funeral or when others have finished their public grieving. Then the child may suddenly change, which is confusing to the parent. *Is his dad's death affecting him a year later? He didn't seem to be that distressed at first.* Well, he may not have been deeply affected at first. Your child probably didn't grieve until he faced the permanency of change the loss brought about.

When children don't understand the permanency of loss, they may not grieve until they are fully impacted by the change the loss brought about.

Attune to Feelings

Children respond in a variety of ways to loss. Sometimes parents are confused by the way their children express their feelings, because children don't respond the way adults do. Because of these differing reactions, parents might assume that their children aren't grieving or aren't affected by the loss. Your children aren't likely to respond in a noticeable way when you tell them something serious. They might continue to play as though you've said nothing. Other children might ask a question that is either unrelated or somewhat relevant but strange or even inappropriate. They might ask more serious questions hours or days later or at the most inopportune times. Be prepared for anything and focus on attuning to your child's feelings before answering or redirecting him.

Rest assured that your child is experiencing an emotional reaction to the news of the great loss. Depending on the age of your child, he may or may not respond with language. Remember, a child's emotions are processed primarily in the emotional brain rather than the thinking brain. Allow your child to react any way he needs to—which includes little to no reaction at all.

Encourage and Educate with Hope

Your child's life has permanently changed and probably not in a good way. More than ever, he needs your support and hopeful assurance. Your child also needs you to teach him about your values. He will be bombarded with all kinds of values regarding death and loss from other people who are well-meaning but who might not share your faith or support him adequately.

Here are some honest and hope-filled things Mary could say to her children.

Be Honest

"We've all been sad for a while."

"I haven't been at my best since Daddy died."

"You haven't been at your best since Daddy died."

Acknowledge Permanent Change

"It's sad that we won't see Daddy in this life again."

"Moving in with Grandma has been hard on us. You've had to share a bedroom with your brother and go to a new school. But it's also been great that Grandma cooks for us every day."

Attune to Feelings

"It's hard for you to get through a day without being mad."

"You really miss Daddy."

"I hear you crying at night sometimes. It's okay to cry as much as you need to. Come get me if you want a hug."

"You feel worried that I might die."

Encourage and Educate with Hope

"We are getting through this day by day."

"God sees our pain, and he cares. He will always provide for us."

"Even though Daddy isn't here on earth, we can still remember him. Let's think of some special ways to remember him."

"You can still talk to Daddy. I believe he hears you and sees you even though you can't hear him or see him."

When Honesty Breaks Your Heart

Mary is now better equipped to speak the unspeakable with her children. She knows *how* to approach communication by understanding each one of her children's language abilities. She knows *what* to say by using an honest but hopeful structure. Of course, she will have to adapt the words and phrases she uses with each child (even drawing pictures for her two youngest if needed), but she feels more confident that her children are going to receive her message.

Even with these tools, speaking the unspeakable to children is really, really hard. Mary is experiencing her own heartbreak, and the details of her husband's death are traumatic. It's okay for Mary to be honest about her own feelings and reactions. It's even okay for her to cry in front of her children, especially if it models a healthy grief response. Mary may choose to write out what she wants to say, and she could plan the communication at a time when she feels stable and ready. She could bring a loved one with her for extra support.

As Christians, we have hope even when the truth is devastating. That hope is of healing, peace, and eternal life. Consider Revelation 21:3-5, a prophecy about the new heaven and new earth:

> I heard a loud voice from the throne saying, "Look! God's dwelling place is now among the people, and he will dwell with them. They will be his people, and God himself will be with them and be their God. 'He will wipe every tear from their eyes. There will be no more death' or mourning

> or crying or pain, for the old order of things has passed away."
>
> He who was seated on the throne said, "I am making everything new!" Then he said, "Write this down, for these words are trustworthy and true."

God's loving truth is this: We always have hope, despite the tragedy of great loss. Someday there will be no more death, mourning, crying, or pain. God is making something new in your child's life, even as you speak.

Jesus,

I long to hear your voice—especially now, when things are so hard. Please speak to me. Help me understand what my child needs to hear. Help me know what to say and how to say it. I want my child to heal, and your voice leads us to healing. As Revelation 21:3-5 tells me, you are making something new in my child and in my family. I hear your words, and I trust they are true.

Amen.

Q: What should I tell my child about traumatic death?

A: Parents wonder if they should be honest with their children about traumatic death, such as suicide, terrorism, and mass casualty events. The answer is, yes, you should be honest. Your child will hear about the event from somewhere (especially the news media), and it is important that you be the primary person to provide reassurance and education to your child. Use the communication principles in this chapter. Be ready for tough questions. Understand that learning about traumatic death might be frightening to your child, so be prepared to provide more hopeful reassurance than usual.

Steps Toward Healing

Draw Strength from This Chapter

- Communicate according to your child's language ability (preverbal, verbal, nonverbal).
- Be honest, address permanent change, attune to your child's feelings, and encourage and educate with hopeful language.
- Find hope in God's Word—it is trustworthy and true.

What You Can Do Right Now

- Pray the chapter prayer over your child.
- Meditate on Ephesians 4:15. Ask the Lord to show you the best way to communicate with your child.
- Reflect on how your child first learned about the great loss. What went well? What didn't? Is there any other information your child might need now? Jot down a few notes.

Activities You Can Do This Week with Your Child

- Plan an intentional check-in time with your child. Use the communication principles in this chapter to talk about how he has been doing since the great loss. If your child does not seem receptive to your check-in, spend time doing something fun together instead. Allow your child to process the great loss his own way and in his own time.
- Set aside a night for you and your child to watch a children's movie that has a grief topic. Here are some suggestions:

Movies for younger children: *The Lion King*, *Finding Nemo*, *Up*
Movies for older children: *Old Yeller*, *My Girl*

Afterward, talk with your child about what he liked and didn't like in the movie. Ask, "Can you relate to the main character or to the story?" These questions might open the door for your child to talk about his loss. Use the skills you learned in this chapter to navigate that conversation.

Tell me the truth with lots of love and hope.

Art by Cynthia, age 9

5

The Really Big Feelings

Wisdom Principle

Loving your child means seeing past the outside.

The Lord *does not look at the things people look at. People look at the outward appearance, but the* Lord *looks at the heart.*

1 Samuel 16:7

"Grandma, I've come to a place of acceptance about my great loss. I was angry at God for a long time, but now I've allowed him to be God and to make the decisions about death and loss. I'd like to apologize for punching a hole in the wall because I was angry. I'll take responsibility for that hole by paying for the repair out of my allowance. I'm ready to move forward with my life. I'm going to set some goals for my growth for this next year. Thank you for supporting me as I work through my grief."

It's almost comical to imagine a child or adolescent making this statement! Children don't think or talk like this. Their brains work much differently from yours or mine. And yet many people expect grieving children to go through grief stages the same way adults do.

Have you heard of the five stages of grief? Theoretically, grieving people experience five emotional states as they resolve their grief. These stages are denial, anger, depression, bargaining, and acceptance. The stages can occur in a linear fashion, or they can occur more randomly.

Ultimately the grieving person comes to a place of acceptance and an ability to move forward.

This theory was developed in the late 1960s by a psychiatrist named Elisabeth Kübler-Ross.[1] It has been an instrumental theory in helping adults work through grief. However, the theory of grief stages doesn't work for children because their thinking brains are still developing. They don't have the insight or the language to identify such complex feelings as denial, bargaining, and acceptance.

The theory of grief stages doesn't work for children because their thinking brains are still developing.

Instead of grief stages, a more accurate way to consider a child's grief is through the lens of attachment theory, which I briefly introduced in chapter 2. Attachment is the ability to bond and to form close relationships. Monitoring children's attachments can help us understand how they are handling grief and loss. Psychologists studied attachment in the mid-twentieth century by observing how infants responded when their primary caregivers left them temporarily. They also studied how infant rhesus monkeys responded when isolated for longer periods of time. In some separations, especially if they were long term or traumatic, the monkey infants' experiences of loss were immediate, all-consuming, and completely impairing. Interestingly, they expressed two primary feelings: instability and despair.

Of course, your child is not a monkey! But attachment studies have given science some insight into emotional and behavioral patterns that might emerge in children who have experienced loss. Take a moment to think about your child's emotional response. Have you noticed distinct grief stages consisting of complex emotions? Probably not. Instead, you've likely noticed that your child seems to feel all kinds of feelings at once. She's different than she was before the great loss—perhaps more agitated or more withdrawn. Her emotions are unpredictable. She's not able to identify her feelings beyond such simple words as mad, sad, or happy. And something deeper seems to be lying underneath the surface...something you can't quite explain. Your child never says it out loud, but you can sense it's there.

Really big feelings—instability and despair.

Instability is expressed outwardly. It is demonstrated through an increase of physical, mental, and emotional agitation, driven by the child's need for security. A child inherently knows she is not yet capable of providing for all her needs, so her great loss renders her helpless (especially if the loss was a parent or caregiver or if the loss also greatly impacted her caregivers). She thus becomes fixated on things that are linked to stability and security. In children, instability can look like an increase in motor activity, behavior problems, ADHD, or even oppositional defiance. It also can look like high anxiety, such as being very worried that her caregivers, siblings, or friends might die. It can manifest in the body through tummy aches, sleep problems, or other signs of physical illness.

In the period immediately after great loss, children usually experience some feelings of instability. If your child's world is in chaos, this is one way she can sort through that chaos. Her emotional radar picks up on the stress around her, and she expresses that stress through disorganized emotion and behavior.

Despair is expressed inwardly. It is demonstrated through a decrease of emotion and physical functioning, which is driven by an internal experience of hopelessness. In children, despair looks like withdrawal, depression, or an emotional shutdown. Extreme despair can sometimes lead to self-harm. Instead of acting out on others through misbehavior, the child turns her pain inward. She may have a hard time expressing any emotion at all, and her behavior may vary between numbness to moody agitation. Suicidal thoughts, self-harm, and negative self-talk can be concerns when children experience deep despair.

Despair often comes after the child's world has been in chaos for a while. Things are never going to be the same again, and she lives life in sadness and hopelessness. In a positive sense, a despairing child has accepted her loss. But the negative side of this acceptance is that the child cannot see her way forward. She can't imagine a future without the lost thing or person.

Children feel grief in two primary ways:
instability and despair.

See Your Child's Heart

The verse that forms the wisdom principle for this chapter is 1 Samuel 16:7: "The LORD does not look at the things people look at. People look at the outward appearance, but the LORD looks at the heart." The prophet Samuel was talking about young David right before he was anointed to be Israel's king. People look at others and make judgments, but the Lord can see the inner heart. On the outside, David appeared to be inadequate for the job of king, but on the inside, his heart was pure.

I think this verse also applies to the feelings of the human heart. We often act one way while feeling another...to cover up the really big feelings that make us vulnerable. People see how we look and act on the outside, and they make judgments about us without having any idea of our feelings deep inside.

Children also cover up their big feelings, but those feelings emerge in other ways, including tearfulness, temper tantrums, angry outbursts, clinginess, back talk, fear, tummy aches, and refusal to sleep alone. They may even become perfectionistic or take on the role of the parent. All these outer feelings are what people can observe. It's good to attune to the outer feelings and intervene if your child needs you to. But to truly reach your child's heart, you must respond to her really big feelings first—before you respond to what you see on the outside. We've arrived at our fifth parenting skill, which is to respond to your child's really big feelings.

PARENTING SKILL

Respond to your child's really big feelings.

Loving your child means seeing past the outside and attending to her heart, especially when it's difficult. Really big emotions are sometimes expressed in unpleasant ways, and they may require correction for misbehavior. These really big feelings are deep and soft and vulnerable. In order to tend to them, you must practice awareness and healing compassion and wisdom. With some practice and intention, you will learn to recognize those deep feelings and respond to them before addressing outward behaviors. Let's look at an example.

Brian, a third grader whose special grandpa died a few months ago, comes home with a failing report card. His teacher commented, "I'm concerned about Brian because his grades are slipping. He is usually a friendly, outgoing kid, but lately he seems withdrawn. He often appears angry or moody. Let me know if there are some ways I can support your family."

Ugh! What a worrisome report for Brian's parent to receive. It would be easy to respond to Brian with alarm or even frustration, but Brian's parent stops and recognizes the really big feelings.

> PARENT: "Hey, Brian, can we talk? I got a note from your teacher today that you're failing in school and having a hard time with the other kids."
>
> BRIAN: "Oh." (*Looks down and says nothing else.*)
>
> PARENT: "What's going on?"
>
> BRIAN: "Nothing."

At this point, Brian's parent knows something is up...a really big feeling. Can you guess which one? Brian is withdrawing, and his grades are failing. His primary feeling is despair. But you see only Brian's outward feelings and behaviors—numbness, slowness, lack of connection, and procrastination. Responding to the external behaviors would be natural, but Brian's parent knows that the outside is merely a manifestation of a really big despair feeling.

> PARENT: "You seem a little sad. It's hard for you to talk to me right now."
>
> BRIAN: "Uh-huh."
>
> PARENT: "It's okay for you to feel sad. You're not in trouble,

Brian. Let's figure this out together. It's important for you to do well in school."

BRIAN: "Why? I hate school."

PARENT: "School is important because it helps you learn things you need to know to be good at life. You have a happy future ahead of you, buddy. I can't wait to see you graduating from high school and starting a job you really love."

BRIAN: "I don't love anything."

PARENT: "I know you haven't figured out what you love yet. That's okay. We've all had a hard time lately. We're going to get through it, and we're going to start with school because that's where we're at right now. I know you can do this. Can you help me think of some things we can do to help you do better in school?"

BRIAN: "Maybe." (Thinks for a minute.) "I don't like sitting in the front where everyone sees me. I want to sit in the back because it's quieter."

Responding to the really big feeling is actually quite simple. You frame your response with the opposites of instability and despair: *stability* and *hope*. If your child displays instability, frame your response with stability. If your child displays despair, frame your response with hope.

Notice how Brian's parent responded to the bad report from the teacher. The parent recognized the big feeling (despair) but never said it out loud. Instead, the parent used hopeful and encouraging language to guide the response, being fully aware that the real issue was not Brian's grades but rather his grief. The response ultimately helped Brian find a solution to his problem, which gave him some mastery over his short-term situation and long-term destiny. The response directed Brian toward hope.

Now let's take a few moments to think about your child. Does she have any feelings or behaviors that could be coming from a deeper place, such as instability or despair? Take a look at the table below, and feel free to jot down a few notes as well.

Big Feeling You Don't See (the Heart)

instability

Outside Feelings You Do See (the Behavior)

agitation

anger

misbehavior directed outside or at others

anxiety exhibited in ritualized behaviors or repetitive questions or statements

panic

separation anxiety

Respond With...

stability

structure

reassurance that your child will be taken care of

reassurance that you are taking care of the child

Big Feeling You Don't See (the Heart)

despair

Outside Feelings You Do See (the Behavior)

sadness

depression

withdrawal
self-harm
anxiety exhibited in ruminating thoughts
isolation

Respond With...

hope
encouragement
assurance that your child will have a good future
permission for your child to move forward into the future

A Foundation of Stability and Hope

Stability and hope are more important for your grieving child than you might think. Take a moment to reflect on the character of God. His true character is rooted in stability and hope. God is the Creator, the Master of intelligent design, the one who set the universe in perfect order (Isaiah 45:12). God is our hope, and he gives us hope through his Son, Jesus, the ultimate hope, our Savior and Healer (Matthew 12:15-21). He never brings confusion (instability) or despair.

One of the most powerful things you can do as a parent is to make God's character qualities of stability and hope the emotional foundation of your home. How might things change if stability and hope formed the basis for everything you did as a parent? How might your child's life change? I encourage you to try it and see what happens.

As an example, every day for the next 30 days, meditate on Isaiah 45:12 and thank God for being a God of stability, hope, and order. Then speak out loud, "In Jesus's name, I claim stability, hope, and order over this household." Meditate on Matthew 12:15-21 and thank God for the gift of his Son, Jesus; for your and your child's redemption; and for your child's healing. Then speak out loud, "In Jesus's name, we are saved, redeemed, and healed. My child's healing is a hope that we are sure of." Let these meditations and affirmations guide your parenting and see how God powerfully transforms your child's feelings of instability and despair into a firm foundation of stability and hope.

Jesus,

I worry about my child sometimes. She has big feelings that I'm not always sure how to handle. But I know that your true nature is stability and hope. In Jesus's name, I claim stability and hope in this home and for my child. Please place your ministering angels around our home and attend to my child's heart. We gladly receive your presence and your peace.

Amen.

Q: What do I do if my child's extreme feelings are not getting any better?

A: Your grieving child's feelings might be extreme, especially if she is starting to show impairment in one or more areas. It's normal to have some minor impairment because of grief, such as problems at school or home. But if your child begins to show moderate to severe impairment, it's time to recruit some extra help. Examples of significant impairment include phobias, refusal to go to school, extreme behavior problems, or suicidal thoughts. Chapter 14 provides some recommendations for working with professional counselors.

Steps Toward Healing

Draw Strength from This Chapter

- Grieving children feel two major emotions—instability and despair.
- You should respond to the heart instead of what you see on the outside.
- God's character is rooted in stability and hope.

What You Can Do Right Now

- Pray the chapter prayer over your child.
- Meditate on 1 Samuel 16:7. Ask God to show you the vulnerable feelings in your child's heart. Ask God for wisdom about how to respond to your child's heart before providing correction.
- Read Matthew 12:15-21. Reflect on times in your life when Jesus healed someone or provided you with hope or stability. Write out one or two short stories about these personal events in child-friendly language.
- Draw a timeline of your child's life from birth to the present. Above the line, note significant events in your child's life, both positive and negative. Under the line, write out significant feelings and behaviors you have noticed. Have your child's feelings and behaviors become more notable after the great loss? What connections do you see? If you decide to elicit spiritual or professional support, this timeline will help you communicate your child's symptoms to the provider.

Activities You Can Do This Week with Your Child

- Read your hopeful life stories out loud to your child. Ask her to write one of her own (younger children may need to draw pictures).
- Model stability to your child. For example, cook dinner together and delegate tasks to your child while you show leadership. Make a commitment to creating an orderly space within your home, and get your child involved in organizing or picking up.
- Practice using hopeful future language with your child. Ask her questions like these (and validate her responses):

  "What do you want to be when you grow up?"

  "What do you think the last day of school is going to feel like this year?"

  "What do you hope to get for your birthday?"

  "What fun activities would you like to do with your own kids someday?"

  "What special jobs has God made you for?"

Art by Annika, age 9

6

The Crazies

Wisdom Principle

Your child's peace is the goal of correction.

No discipline seems pleasant at the time, but painful. Later on, however, it produces a harvest of righteousness and peace for those who have been trained by it.

Hebrews 12:11

Daddy, can I have a candy bar? Can I have a candy bar? Why not? I DON'T CARE if it's not good for me. I want it. It's okay to have a little chocolate—you even said so! Can I have it? WHY NOT! YOU'RE MEAN, DADDY! MOMMY ALWAYS LET ME HAVE IT!"

It's all Trevon can do to hold himself together. He's now a single dad parenting two kids. He's working full-time and running back and forth from school to day care to soccer practice to playdates to birthday parties...all while trying to keep a reasonably clean house and food on the table.

And he could do it all...if only his kids would behave.

Trevon's biggest surprise about parenting alone was that managing small children in a crowded supermarket, with everyone staring at them (probably judging his parenting skills—or worse, feeling sorry for him), is a megachallenge. It's not easy being Dad *and* Mom, and Trevon feels like one gigantic, lonely failure.

His kids aren't faring well either. More and more, they have meltdowns that are painfully intense, utterly uncalled for, and completely disproportionate to the situation. I call these meltdowns "the crazies," and I bet you know exactly what the crazies are. Irrational and unpredictable moments when your child simply refuses to do what he knows is right. All the good stuff you've taught him dissolves at the sight of a Hershey bar.

Of course, all children succumb to the crazies. It's part of childhood. Misbehavior and the subsequent correction help children learn how to navigate the world in a healthy way. But parents of grieving children often wonder, *Are the crazies normal childhood behavior, or are they a way for grief to eke its way out?* Even the most well-intentioned parent may pause before enforcing limits. *He's hurting so much. Will discipline break my grieving child's heart even more?*

The Candy Bar Could Worsen the Grief

It would be so tempting for Trevon to give in on the candy bar. It would get him out of the store in peace, just squeaking in enough time to get the groceries loaded into the car before kid number two hits the crazies. And his son would know Trevon's love for him. *Perhaps a little chocolate would soothe his pain. Maybe we all should have a candy bar! After all, we've all been through so much...*

It's easy to excuse, overlook, or give in to your grieving child's misbehavior. Guilt or compassion might push you to say yes when your discipline principles say no. But deep down, you know that failing to parent your child's misbehavior will cause him more problems in the long run. Your child must be prepared for life, which means he needs to learn important skills, such as refraining from impulse buys, not soothing his pain with food or substances, and practicing healthy nutrition. Right now, the stakes are low with the candy bar. But if your child does not learn to delay gratification, he will eventually face much higher consequences.

Trevon is aware of the bigger picture, so he stands firm in saying no to the candy bar despite his child's verbal barrage. It's pretty tough, but it's the right thing to do—and not only because kids need to learn self-control. Setting boundaries with grieving children is critical for another reason: Failing to correct your child's misbehavior could *worsen* his grief.

Remember the really big feelings? Consider the really big feeling of instability. Instability threatens a child's sense of safety and security. Children who feel unstable fear that no one is going to take care of them. This creates a lot of anxiety, which can cause the child to act out. Setting boundaries lets your child know he doesn't have to take care of himself. There is a loving, stable adult who will take care of him. He may resist the limits you set, but ultimately the boundary sends a message to your child's heart that he can relax. Someone else is in charge.

Children who are experiencing despair feel very alone. Setting a boundary lets them know someone else is there. Someone sees him and notices what is happening. The despairing child may resist the boundary just like the child who is sensing instability. Nonetheless, continue to set standards for his behavior and enforce them. If you, the parent who is supposed to love him unconditionally, don't use these situations to build a stronger connection and facilitate growth, your despairing child has few options to help him connect with others and move forward in life.

Ultimately the boundary sends a message
to your child's heart that he can relax.
Someone else is in charge.

The really big feelings are overwhelming—both for you and your child—but the antidote is not to give your child more disorganization (lack of boundaries) or despair (lack of attention). The antidote is to give your child structure and opportunities to grow. Correction and discipline are critical. You cannot let them slide even though your child is grieving.

Heart Attendance

It's going to happen—I guarantee it. Like Trevon, you are going to have to correct your child...and you might even have to do it in a crowded supermarket with everyone watching. It might seem like an overwhelming task, but here's a simple principle to use when correcting a grieving child. We have arrived at our sixth parenting skill, which is to attend to your child's heart before providing correction.

PARENTING SKILL

Attend to your child's heart before providing correction.

Your child's misbehavior is wound up in grief. His heart is broken, so your long-term goal is to help Jesus mend his broken heart. How can you discipline him in a way that puts his heart back together rather than breaking it even further?

As the parent, you can make a logical connection between your child's misbehavior and his great loss. However, your child cannot yet make that connection. Here's an example:

(*Child draws on the wall using permanent markers.*)

PARENT: "*Why* did you do that? You know you're not supposed to draw on the wall with your markers!"

CHILD: "I don't know."

PARENT: "This behavior is inappropriate. I am taking the markers away, and you are taking a time-out!"

CHILD: "I hate you! You're mean!"

PARENT: "You can't talk to me like that. Is this about your mother's death?"

CHILD: "I hate you! *You're not my mom!*"

PARENT: "Go to your room, young lady! And don't come out until I tell you!"

(*Child runs into her room, slams the door, and begins destroying everything in sight.*)

While the parent is spot-on that the child's grief has jammed bad behavior into sixth gear, this interaction didn't work well. In fact, the parent's correction just seemed to make the child's feelings and behavior worse. The parent failed to attend to the child's heart. Here's what the parent could have done differently:

(*Child draws on the wall using permanent markers.*)

PARENT: "*Why* did you do that? You know you're not supposed to draw on the wall with your markers!"

CHILD: "I don't know."

PARENT: "It's not okay to draw on the wall with your markers. Markers are for using with paper. I'm wondering what you were feeling when you decided to draw on the wall with your markers."

CHILD: "I don't know."

PARENT: "Hmm. I wonder if you were feeling mad? Or scared, or sad?"

CHILD: "I was mad."

PARENT: "What were you mad about?"

CHILD: "Another kid at school took the last chocolate milk, and I didn't get any."

PARENT: "You felt mad that you missed out on the chocolate milk today. I'm sorry that happened. It's not okay to use your mad feelings to make a bad choice, especially a choice that hurts others, like our family or our home. I will enforce a consequence, and I'm going to need to think about that consequence for a while. For now, I'd like you to go to your room to take a time-out. Think about how you might make a different choice next time when you're mad."

CHILD: (*Looks down.*) "I'm sorry." (*Goes to room.*)

This time the parent didn't bring up the great loss, and the parent attended to the child's heart. The parent asked about the child's feelings and empathized with the child's sad feeling of missing out on something important. Then the parent briefly and concretely explained why the child's behavior was not okay and enforced a consequence.

Bringing up the great loss during discipline—especially in the really tense moments—is not effective. The great loss might be the deeper issue lurking underneath the surface, but it is not the issue you need to deal with in the moment. Furthermore, if you bring it up to your child during discipline, he is likely to feel anger and shame over the great loss as well as shame over his behavior. He feels misunderstood. He begins to feel resentful and angry, and he will likely direct his angry feelings at you, the one who he perceives is creating more uncomfortable feelings for him.

Attending to the heart means understanding how grief is impacting your child's behavior. You use this understanding to frame your correction, but you focus on what is happening in the moment (your child's behavior). It is absolutely okay—and even important—to talk about the great loss with your child. Just do so when your child is calm and open. Let your child bring it up and talk about it on his own terms. As he grows older, he will be able to make deeper connections between his loss and how it affects the way he thinks, feels, and behaves, especially if he has been allowed to do so in a safe and peaceful way.

A broken heart hurts. Discipline that is reactive or shaming or that triggers feelings of grief breaks your child's heart even more. Discipline that attends to the heart is effective and necessary.

The great loss might be the deeper issue lurking underneath your child's misbehavior, but it is not the issue you need to deal with in the moment.

Keep Walking Though the Journey Is Long

You are well into your journey toward healing. I'm sure it's been a long journey. And it probably feels like you have such a long way to go. The author of Hebrews understood that exhaustion too. Take a few moments to turn to Hebrews 12 now. Read verses 1-13. Do you notice anything? The author of Hebrews starts off the chapter with encouragement for a long race. Sometimes parenting through grief feels like a long, exhausting race...especially if you are dealing with the crazies. But through discipline—both the discipline you give to your child as well as your self-discipline to parent well through this season—there is a beautiful promise of healing:

> Therefore, strengthen your feeble arms and weak knees. "Make level paths for your feet" so that the lame may not be disabled, but rather healed (verses 12-13).

We are to strengthen ourselves and move forward, and we do so to overcome. God doesn't want us to be disabled (brokenhearted); he wants us to be healed. Despite the discomfort or the difficulty of disciplining your child in the moment, God assures you that loving discipline eventually will be one of the pathways to your child's healing.

Jesus,

Sometimes I feel so frustrated at my child's behavior. I am at a loss as to what to do. I welcome your presence and wisdom, especially in the really tough moments. Help me slow down, stay calm, and attend to my child's heart before providing correction. Help me stand firm with good boundaries that will help my child grow into a whole, healed adult. You are a strong, resolute father and a nurturing, empathetic mother. I receive your guidance and support.

Amen.

Q: What are some simple, heart-attending responses for my child's misbehavior?

A:

- "I love you too much to let you think that behavior is okay."

- "I understand you're sad. But it's not okay to use your sad feelings as a reason to hurt others."
- "It's not okay for you to talk to me like that. It *is* okay for you to feel mad, but we use kind words even when we're mad. Please try again."
- "We're both going to take a time-out. We'll try again when you're ready to be kind."
- "Toys [*or* our house/my property/the pets] are not for hurting. I am going to remove them [*or* you] until you can be safe."
- You can choose to ignore a child who is having a temper tantrum or angry outburst. Comment out loud, "I'll be ready to listen when you are ready to be kind." Give your attention back to the child when he begins behaving appropriately. (Don't ignore a child who is being physically aggressive or destructive. In this case, you should remove the child to a safe place until he de-escalates. If the child refuses to leave or is too big to pick up, then remove other children, property, and yourself until he is calm.)

Steps Toward Healing

Draw Strength from This Chapter

- Failure to correct your child's misbehavior could worsen your child's grief.
- Correction should be provided only after you attend to your child's heart.
- Discipline rooted in God's wisdom will lead to your child's healing (Hebrews 12:11-13).

What You Can Do Right Now

- Pray the chapter prayer over your child.
- Read Hebrews 12:1-13. Identify one verse that will help when you are tired or need encouragement. Memorize that verse or write it down somewhere. Meditate on that verse when you need it.
- Reflect on your foundational parenting principles. Journal answers to these questions:

1. Ask yourself what principles provide the foundation for your parenting. (Identify verses in the Bible if you can, or look up some verses if you need to develop foundational parenting principles.)
2. Ask yourself what you need to change so that your discipline proactively leads to righteousness, peace, and healing for your child.
3. Imagine your child as an adult, fully healed from his grief and loss. Ask the Holy Spirit to guide your imagining. What kind of character qualities would your child have? Pray over your child, asking for those qualities throughout

the week and beyond: "In faith and through the power of Jesus Christ, I speak out loud that [child's name] will be [character quality]." Ask the Lord for wisdom on how you can develop those qualities in your child.

Activities You Can Do This Week with Your Child

- Read Hebrews 12:11 out loud to your child. Explain what the verse means. Ask your child to think about what his life would be like if he made good choices and had peace in his heart. What would he do and say? What would he think and feel? Write down his answers. Then pray together, "Dear Jesus, help me make good choices. Thank you for healing my heart. Amen."
- Help your child practice self-discipline. Get a large piece of paper and think about house rules (ways of living with each other that bring peace). Have your child write them down. Post the house rules where everyone can see them. This process helps your child take ownership over his behavior and to see the importance of kindness in a family.

Art by Annika, age 9

7

It's So Messed Up

When Your Teen Is Grieving

Wisdom Principle

Teens need meaningful identity outside their great loss.

"I know the plans I have for you," declares the LORD, *"plans to prosper you and not to harm you, plans to give you hope and a future."*

JEREMIAH 29:11

Rachel was 15 years old when the unthinkable happened. Waking up at a friend's house one Saturday morning, she got a text that changed her life forever. *Come home right now. They're looking for your boyfriend and can't find him.* Rachel had a sinking feeling in the pit of her stomach—her boyfriend had been depressed off and on. She thought he was okay, but he wasn't. When she got home, Rachel's father told her that the boyfriend had completed suicide. Rachel's life was changed forever.

It wasn't just that her boyfriend died or that he died in a horrible and unexpected way. It was how his death affected the way people saw her for the rest of her high school years. Rachel became "the girlfriend of the kid who died." The girl that everyone tiptoed around because they were afraid of upsetting her. Some boys didn't want to date her because they were threatened by her remembrance of her deceased boyfriend. Other boys avoided her because they felt unable to measure up to his memory.

Adults, who should have known better, weren't much help either. Some bombarded her with information about grief. Others smothered her with concern about her own physical safety. Many stayed away from her when she really needed someone to listen. Rachel went through her high school years in a shroud of heaviness. Her identity was wrapped up in her great loss, and she couldn't break out of it. In her despair, Rachel became depressed and even considered suicide herself.

How did Rachel describe her great loss? "It was just so messed up."

They Are Not Just Hormonal

Close your eyes for a moment. How would you feel if you were strapped into a roller coaster for ten years and couldn't get off no matter how hard you tried? This is what it feels like to parent a teenager under normal circumstances. The only consistent thing is the inconsistency—sweet and sickening ups and downs. But as you well know by now, grief turns a normal-sized roller coaster into a megawild ride, complete with loops of logic, tearful waterworks, and explosive mood pyrotechnics.

Whew. I'm tired just thinking about it!

Dear parent, I know you must be tired too. And you're very concerned about your grieving teenager. Let's take a moment out of your journey to rest. I have some encouraging news for you. Rachel is now a young adult who made it through some incredibly difficult teenage years. And I am delighted to tell you that Jesus is healing her in amazing ways.

He's going to do that same amazing healing for your child.

And that healing is going to start in your home. Yes, you're in for a wild ride...for a while. But so is your teen. She's strapped into that emotional roller coaster right along with you.

Teens have significant mood swings because their brains and bodies are changing rapidly. Their bodies are producing hormones that prepare them for reproduction and adulthood. Their thinking brains are growing like crazy, which means that they have more existential questions about the world, the meaning of life, their identity, and the like.

At the same time, they make most of their decisions with the emotional brain, which means they don't always make rational choices. They desire a lot of freedom, but they still need full provision and protection.

Under the best of circumstances, you can expect your teen to experience very high highs and very low lows with no apparent pattern. When grief is buckled into the ride too, your teen's nervous system becomes even more overloaded, and her mood and behavior become even more irrational and unpredictable.

Is it grief, or is it hormones? It's both. Your teen is experiencing the normal mood swings of adolescence plus 100 layers of grief. The bottom line is that it doesn't really matter if it's hormones or grief. What matters is that your teen is having an intense experience, and she needs your support to get through it.

Your teen doesn't yet have the life experience to know the ride will end someday. You do. So all along this wild ride, your teen needs your encouragement. Communicate this to your teen: "Things are really messed up right now, but they won't be forever. You are going to get through this, and you are going to be even stronger." Encourage your teen with this language as often as she needs it.

Your teen's struggle could very well pull your heartstrings so much, you stop parenting. But your teen needs your guidance through her grief. Great loss doesn't cancel out the need for growth. She needs you to continue to provide boundaries, correction, and direction. However, she also needs you to recognize the deep impact of her great loss and to attune to her feelings while she processes it. In chapter 6, you learned how to attend to your child's heart before providing correction, direction, or intervention. Now you can practice attending to your teen's heart.

Don't... react to your teen's emotions with alarm or anger.

Do... expect more intense emotions, practice attuned responses, and attend to your own self-care so you can manage a long season of difficult interactions with your child.

Don't... stop parenting because you feel sorry for your teen.

Do... continue to enforce boundaries and expectations, but first attend to the heart, and take more time with your teen to rest, breathe, and connect.

Friend or Parent?

Have you ever eaten something that didn't sit so well in your stomach? The remedy is to give your body time to digest the bad food and get it out of your system before you eat again. Acute grief and loss also require waiting and processing. In the first weeks following her great loss, Rachel faced a challenge: People bombarded her with information. Well-meaning friends and family visited her because they cared. But ultimately their encouragement and comfort overloaded her system. She was overwhelmed, and she couldn't process anything new. She needed time to rest and digest the bad stuff until she was ready to take in more.

If your teen or family has experienced a trauma like Rachel's, you know the overwhelming feelings of shock, loss, and deep pain your child is feeling. In the immediate aftermath of a loss, parents just don't know what to say or what to do. Nor should you be expected to...parents aren't usually trained to be emergency responders.

But here's the good news: You don't have to say anything or do anything. Do your best to control your teen's environment to facilitate rest, even if that means turning people away for a while. Your teen may want to be alone or stay home. Is this something to worry about? No—this quiet time is a normal stress response that the body and the mind need to recover. Allow your teen this time and space, but watch over her peacefully so you can be there when she's ready for you. And when she is, it's time to listen. This leads to our next parenting skill: Listen but don't stop parenting.

PARENTING SKILL

Listen but don't stop parenting.

Teens often get *talked at* rather than *listened to*. Listening seems so simple, but it's one of the biggest parent-child struggles during the teen years. As a parent, you know that your number one job is to teach your teen to be a self-sufficient adult who loves God. Parents often teach by talking and modeling, which works with younger children. But now that your child has reached adolescence, she needs a different style of teaching. She learns best when she succeeds and fails through her own efforts. She needs space to figure out things on her own. And she needs a support system in place to catch her if she falls.

Instead of talking, quietly take in what your teen is saying. Then ask her questions that will prompt her to think critically. This approach will help your teen think in more complex ways and come up with solutions to her own problems. Here are some examples:

- Instead of saying, "*Why* did you do that?" try asking, "How did that work out for you?"
- Instead of providing a solution to a problem or challenge, try asking, "What do you think is the best thing to do about that?" If you don't think your teen's solution is a great one, allow her to go through with it anyway and count it as a learning experience. Simply say, "I hope that works out for you. Let me know if you need support or want to think through plan B." (The only exception is if you believe your teen's solution would harm her or others or bring about negative long-term consequences. In that case, intervene with a solution or limit.)
- Instead of asking, "How are you doing about [the great loss]," try asking, "What's one big thing you've learned in the past few [weeks/months]?"

Here are a few simple tips for good listening: Talk less than the other person. Stop what you are doing and make eye contact. Smile and relax your face with a kind expression. Reflect on what your teen is saying before responding with your own thoughts. Try to see the feeling or need behind what your teen is saying. Point out that feeling in an affirmative way: "I hear that you don't want to go to school tomorrow."

"You feel like the other kids are talking about you behind your back." "You were embarrassed in health class today when the teacher was talking about depression." "I appreciate you sharing your feelings with me. That was very brave."

Good listeners talk less than the other person.

Now we're ready to consider the difference between being your teen's friend and being her parent. Friends would be good listeners—and that's all. Parents listen well but also set and enforce boundaries that help their teens grow into healthy, self-sufficient adults: "It's important that you go to school despite how difficult it's been. As an adult, you'll have to do things you don't want to do, and I wouldn't be doing you any favors by letting you stay home because I would be teaching you to avoid doing hard things when they feel bad. So let's find a solution together. Since you're almost an adult, I'd like you to come up with some potential solutions. We'll talk through them and decide on the best one for you. And then I will support you as you move forward."

Don't... repeatedly ask your teen how she's doing or bombard her with information about grief recovery.

Do... ask your teen to do something with you that she enjoys, plan regular dates where you can have fun and where your teen can feel normal, and allow your teen to bring up the great loss spontaneously—and be ready to listen when she does.

Don't... force her to talk about the great loss with you.

Do... ask questions that spark critical thinking, and when she wants to talk to you, be ready to listen.

Don't... baby talk, minimize feelings, ignore behaviors you deem attention seeking, or talk to your teen the same way you talk to her younger siblings.

Do... talk to your teen the way you would talk to an adult, show empathy and respect for feelings, and enforce boundaries with hopeful language that helps her move forward.

They Just Want to Feel Normal

Do you remember your teen years? The awkwardness, the confusion? Just wanting to fit in and be cool? Your teen wants to feel that way too. But nothing is normal about great loss. Now everything's messed up. More than ever, your teen needs to find ways to feel normal. She needs your support. Encourage her to remain involved in everyday things, such as school, extracurricular activities, and peer relationships. You don't want to discount the great loss, but your encouragement helps your teen move forward...just like all the other kids her age.

Guess what else makes your teen feel normal? She might not want to talk to you about her great loss. Instead, she may prefer to talk to her friends or other adults. I know this is incredibly difficult because you want to be the one to support your teen. But her desire to elicit support from other people is part of the normal developmental process of adolescence. Your teen is forming her own identity, which means she needs to discover who she is outside of her relationship with you and her other family members. It's painful, yes. But it's an important process for your teen. If she separates successfully and forms her own identity, you have a good chance of having a healthy relationship with her when she's an adult. Your adult child will be self-sufficient and relate to you as an adult rather than as a child.

Your teen is going to seek out support, consciously or not. Here is where you can weave in a little parental wisdom. Help your teen find resources that are healthy, positive, and congruent with your faith. Elicit help from a youth pastor, a professional counselor, or other trusted adults. Encourage your teen to develop relationships with peers that will lead her down a positive path rather than a negative one.

Encourage her to participate in positive activities, such as church and extracurriculars that help her feel good about herself. And don't forget to pray for your teen as often as possible.

Small steps, day after day. Your teen may be walking slowly, but she will be moving toward her healing. Jeremiah 29:11 confirms that despite the challenges of one's situation, God's ultimate plan is for hope and a good future. Rachel chose to embrace God's hope and plan for her future. She had many difficult, painful days, but Jesus helped her see that he had planned more for her than great loss.

Rachel learned that there is a difference between *being* messed up and *feeling* messed up. Being messed up has to do with identity; feeling messed up is a normal response to a terrible situation. Ultimately Jesus helped Rachel see that her identity was in him, and she trusted God to turn her mess into something beautiful.

Jesus mended Rachel's broken heart. Today, she is an independent young woman, working to establish a career and healthy, lifelong relationships.

Because of Jesus, life's losses don't define your teen. They are part of her history, yes. But they are never *who she is*. Help your teen discover exactly who she is—a child of the living God, full of favor, overflowing with grace, and blessed with a promise for a hopeful future.

Don't... expect to be the main source of support for your teen.

Do... remember teens naturally seek solace in their friends, and encourage healthy peer relationships.

Don't... isolate your teen in your family.

Do... encourage your teen to connect with healthy, supportive relationships inside and outside your family and helpful resources such as a youth pastor, youth group, professional counselor, school counselor, or mentor.

Don't...be alarmed if your teen has a spiritual or emotional crisis. Expect these developmental crises as a normal part of working through great loss.

Do...pray for your teen daily and help your teen find her identity and meaning outside of the great loss.

Jesus,

My teen's world has been rocked to its very core. She just wants to feel normal again. I ask you to heal my grieving teenager. She has a lot of questions, and I'm not sure how to answer them. I'm not sure how to provide her the support she needs right now. Please give me wisdom. Help me find the right resources for her. Please move toward her where she's at even though her emotions are so up and down. Be close to her. I know that you will never let her go, and I trust you are leading her to a bright future.

Amen.

Q: What if my teen becomes suicidal?

A: Parents may worry that their grieving teens will experience so much despair that they become severely depressed or have suicidal thoughts. It could happen, but don't assume that it will. The signs to watch for are significant isolation, major changes in behavior, self-harm, outward expressions of suicidal thoughts or plans, or other significant life impairment. Carefully watch over your teen without being pushy. Check in often, interact with her friends, and regularly monitor her social media posts. If you are concerned about your teen's mental health or physical safety, it's time to get some professional help. Chapter 14 will give you some support.

Steps Toward Healing

Draw Strength from This Chapter

- Teens experience grief like a roller coaster. The ups and downs can last a long time.
- More than anything else, grieving teens need parents to listen.
- Your teen needs help connecting to healthy support systems.
- Your teen needs help finding identity outside of the great loss.

What You Can Do Right Now

- Pray the chapter prayer over your teen.
- Meditate on Jeremiah 29:11. Ask God to give you a picture of your teen's *hope* and *future*. Write down whatever God gives you. Do this daily and keep a journal. When your teen seems open (even if a lot of time has passed), share your journal with her.

Activities You Can Do This Week with Your Child

- Invite your teen on a date to do something she enjoys. Explain that your special time will be casual and not focused on "the messed-up stuff." Do your best to attend to your teen and listen to her. This is not a time to provide direction but a time to give your teen an opportunity to feel normal, special, and listened to.
- Invite some of your teen's friends over. Make something in the kitchen together—homemade pizza, cookies, BBQ, or something else they enjoy. If they're not into cooking,

play some games or sports outside. Put on some fun music, laugh, and share stories. Take lots of selfies and pictures with your phone. Even if they pretend to be too cool or uninterested, they will have a good time and feel loved and cared for by a stable adult.

- If you have younger children in your home who also are grieving, show your teen this book and ask her to read it (or parts of it). She may learn some concepts that will help her grieve without feeling like you are bombarding her with information. Ask your teen to support you in your efforts to help her younger siblings grieve. Teens gain a sense of purpose when they are a healthy role model for others. However, be careful not to abdicate your parental role in this approach. Your teen still needs her own time, space, and way to grieve. She needs you to be the parent, ultimately facilitating the grieving process in your home.

Art by Elowynn, age 17

8

Saying Goodbye to Someone Special

Wisdom Principle

Children need hopeful and accurate information to say goodbye.

Guide me in your truth and teach me,
for you are God my Savior,
and my hope is in you all day long.

Psalm 25:5

In the early morning of September 6, 1997, I was engrossed in one of the most memorable funerals I've ever seen. I had traded sleep to sit in my living room and say goodbye to the Princess Diana of Wales. Brokenhearted people lined the streets, weeping and leaving their remembrances of their beloved princess. But it was seeing her sons, Princes William and Harry, that unlocked my tears. They bravely marched behind their mother's casket, trying not to let their faces break...I ached for those boys. I wondered if they wanted to say goodbye to their mother with the world watching or if they just went along with everything because they were expected to.

Saying goodbye to someone special is an intense experience. Responses are fraught with unpredictability, both yours and others'. You feel so many things all at once—shock, sadness, fear, even relief or peace—and yet a pervading numbness makes it hard to feel anything at all. Putting all your feelings into words is nearly impossible, so you just cry and try your best to get through it.

Imagine, then, what saying goodbye is like for your child.

Saying Goodbye

Like adults, children need to say goodbye when someone special is gone forever. Not only does saying goodbye help your child process acute grief; it also teaches your child that it is important to process grief in healthy ways. I'm sure you sense the importance of your child's need to say goodbye. But the thought of navigating a funeral or other memorial might provoke a lot of anxiety and questions for you. What does your child need, and where do you start? We have arrived at the next step in your journey, which is to lovingly educate and support your child as he says goodbye. Your special assignment is to help your child say goodbye in his own meaningful way.

PARENTING SKILL

Lovingly educate and support your child as he says goodbye.

Funerals or memorial services are the most culturally public ways of saying goodbye. Sometimes they can be challenging for children, especially if the memorial is your child's first exposure to death. Parents might be unsure how to involve their children in the memorial, but including them in the process is important. Here are a few principles that will help you navigate this event.

Tell your child what is going to happen.

Death memorials contain many different rituals and expressions that can be new to children. They also can be traumatic experiences for children, especially if they are not prepared. Sit down with your child and explain what is going to happen. If your child is young, you might want to have some art supplies handy so you can sketch a picture for him or have your child draw a picture showing what he thinks is going to happen. Educate your child about new words or concepts, such as casket, viewing, funeral service, hearse, burial, wake, and cremation. If you think your child might experience anything that will scare or worry him, such as other people's displays of grief, prepare your child ahead of time and encourage him: "It's okay to cry and show others how we feel at Grandpa's funeral. Everybody says goodbye in their own special way, including you. We will do our best to understand and comfort others, and we will receive comfort from others too."

Allow your child to participate in whatever way he wishes.

Children are members of the family and need to be included in all family events, including memorials. However, a memorial might be a new or scary experience for your child, so encourage him to participate—or not participate—the way he would like to. Let your child know whether other family members plan to do special things at the memorial. Ask your child if he would like to do anything special to say goodbye. Honor what your child does, and ask other family members to be respectful. (Sometimes adults think children are cute or sweet, and they react to children's participation with laughter or smiles during serious moments. Let adult family members know about your child's desired participation ahead of time in a way that will help them remember to take your child seriously.)

Your child needs to say goodbye in his own special way. Don't force your child to do anything he doesn't want to do. Well-intentioned adults might have ideas about how children should participate, but your child's greatest need is to say goodbye in his own way. You can give your child suggestions, but in the end, let your child make his own decision about participating.

Your child needs to say goodbye in his own special way.

Don't force your child to attend the memorial if he doesn't want to.

Since a memorial is a family event, you should assume your child will attend. Don't give him the option. However, your child might express on his own that he does not want to attend. If this happens, ask your child why he does not want to attend. If his reason is based on fear or discomfort, do your best to lovingly educate him about why saying goodbye is important. Ask your child what you can do to help him be more comfortable. For example, perhaps he could attend the memorial service but not view the body in an open casket. However, if he absolutely does not want to go, don't force him. Forcing a child to attend a memorial can do more harm than good if he feels afraid or cannot process a personal goodbye in a public way.

Consider facilitating a personal goodbye later with your child.

The public memorial is designed to meet the needs of a family and community. Your child might not be able to have the goodbye process he fully needs, or he might feel lost in the crowd. Your child might have a delayed grief reaction, or his brain might be so full taking in a new experience that he isn't able to experience his own sad feelings. Consider facilitating a special goodbye later if your child needs it, especially if he chose not to attend the memorial. Chapter 9 has a few ideas for facilitating a goodbye ceremony.

Help your child understand that acute grief is not permanent.

Acute grief is all-consuming. It can be scary and filled with despair, especially if this is your child's first great loss. The loss is permanent, but the acute (immediate, intense) grieving of that loss is not. Lovingly encourage your child, explaining that he won't always feel this sad: "It hurts a lot right now because we miss Grandpa so much. It's okay to feel sad. But our hearts will heal, and we won't always feel so sad. There will be happier days. Let's trust Jesus to heal our broken hearts in his perfect time." Don't minimize your child's feelings of acute grief; instead, validate them and allow him to feel them. Acknowledge that he will always feel some sadness about his loss, but provide hope that his heart won't always hurt as much as it does right now.

Special Support for Special Losses

Children respond to the losses of people and pets in special ways. Here are some concepts that will help you support children who are working through unique losses.

The Death or Loss of a Pet

For children, the death of a cherished pet can be just as hard as the death of a person. Pets offer unconditional love, and caring for a pet is often a child's first opportunity to practice responsibility and empathy. The death of a pet is not always acknowledged as a real death in the family, and that can lead to unresolved grief in children. You can help your child during such a time by acknowledging the significance of this loss. When you guide your child through a mourning process for the death of a pet, he will learn that grieving is important and necessary for healing and moving on. He'll also learn healthy coping strategies for other losses he will experience in his life.[1]

The Death of a Grandparent

The death of a grandparent often is the first experience children have of someone close to them dying. Death becomes real. Children become aware of mortality (including their own), especially if they had a close relationship with the grandparent. The new awareness of their mortality can make children feel anxious, and that anxiety can increase if parents can't attune to it. (Children's needs often go overlooked during the business of funeral arrangements and estate administration.)

When a grandparent dies, children lose a source of unconditional love. It's a double loss if the grandparent was a primary caretaker for a child—in that case, it's as if the child lost a parent too. Parents can help children who are mourning the loss of a grandparent by ensuring that their children's needs are met during acute grieving and beyond. Even if you are busy making arrangements or dealing with your own grief, take some special time with your child every day (even 15 minutes will make a difference). Attune to your child's emotional responses and questions. Be ready to answer questions about death and dying. (See "Answers to Tough Theological Questions About Death and Loss" on page 199.)

The Death of a Peer

Approximately one in every 1,500 children dies before reaching adulthood.[2] Thus your child is likely to have at least one peer who dies—a friend, cousin, classmate, or sibling—before his eighteenth birthday. Most children can grasp the death of pets or older adults, but the death of a peer can rock your child's world. Death becomes very real, and it can provoke additional fears in your child: *Will I be next? Can my family get into an accident? Can I get sick?* If your child has lost a peer, you can help by normalizing his fears and reassuring him that he is safe.[3] Assure him that you will always look out for his needs and that God will watch over him: "I hear you are afraid that you could die. It is true that we all will die someday, but we don't have to be afraid of death. You are healthy, and we live our lives in safe ways. We can trust God to take care of us. We choose to live our lives in faith and not fear." Then model living your life full of faith and not in fear! Your child will learn more from your example than your words.

The Death of an Immediate Family Member

The hardest goodbye can come when someone who lives in your child's home passes away. Since the deceased is usually a parent, caregiver, or sibling, your child will experience a great deal of shock in the days and weeks after the death, even if the death was expected. In these situations, children almost always need an intentional mourning season and their own personal goodbye in addition to the public memorial.

Parents can help children who have lost an immediate family member by not pressuring them to say goodbye on everyone else's schedule. Allow your child time to rest, breathe, and connect...time for his nervous system to recover. In time, and when your child seems open to it, begin to introduce the idea of saying a personal goodbye. See chapter 9 for more detail on facilitating an intentional mourning season.

Parents can help children who have lost an immediate family member by not pressuring them to say goodbye on everyone else's schedule.

A Healthy Goodbye

In counseling, the goodbye process between the therapist and client is just as important as the rest of the therapy—in fact, the goodbye is part of the therapy! In my work as a mental health counselor, I've discovered that many people don't know how to say goodbye. It's not something we learn until we have to or we intentionally decide to. Pause for a moment to think about this. Did anyone ever teach you how to say goodbye to someone special in a healthy way? How have the goodbyes in your life gone? Have they been healing? Have they brought you peace?

Many of our goodbyes in life are not peaceful. In fact, they often are filled with sadness, confusion, disappointment, and anger. This is why goodbyes are usually considered unpleasant or are avoided altogether. This is also why navigating a goodbye after a death or loss can be awkward. But a peaceful, healthy goodbye is possible, both for you and your child. As in therapy, a healthy goodbye to someone special becomes part of the healing process. It also becomes a life skill for navigating future relationships. Here are a few principles for healthy goodbyes:

- Recognize that the relationship has ended or changed.
- Acknowledge the specialness of the relationship.
- Share and celebrate memories or milestones.
- Share what is going to be hard about not sharing day-to-day life with the person.
- Share your hopes for yourself and for the other person.
- Say goodbye.

Regardless of whether your child participates in the public memorial, work through these principles with him to help him say goodbye. You don't have to work through all of them at once. What language would you use with your child? What questions would you ask him? How might he react to them?

Goodbye for Now

Wise parents provide education about death and memorials. Accurate information, yes, but accurate information presented in a hopeful way. Psalm 25:5 says, "Guide me in your truth and teach me, for you are God my Savior, and my hope is in you all day long." In this verse we are reminded that God speaks truth to us, even though that truth might be difficult. Or scary. Or traumatic. But knowing the truth helps us feel stable, and it helps us trust God.

The same is true for your child when you speak the truth to him. And the truth is, death is not the end for Christians. Death on earth is a new beginning in heaven. We are saying goodbye for now but not goodbye forever.

Jesus,

My child is facing one of life's hardest challenges—saying goodbye. I invite your presence into this process, Jesus. Show up for him, walk beside him, hold him, and comfort him. Help him face this intense experience with bravery. Give him the confidence that you are healing his heart, even in this very moment.

Amen.

Q: What if my child didn't get to say a special goodbye?

A: You may be reading this book years after your child's great loss, and looking back, you might wonder if your child actually had a chance to say goodbye in his own meaningful way. Memorials occur within weeks of a death, and the time leading up to the memorial is overflowing with planning, details, and working with extended family. A child's needs might not be the first priority during this time. (This can be expected. There is no shame about this—it just happens.) After the public memorial, life might have been busy with new adjustments or just simply trying to move on. Now might be a good time to slow down, reflect on how your child reacted during that time, and talk about it with your child. If your child would like to do his own special goodbye now, offer to walk him through it.

Help me say goodbye in my own special way.

Steps Toward Healing

Draw Strength from This Chapter

- Help your child say goodbye in his own special way.
- Provide special support to your child during the public memorial.
- Provide special support for goodbyes to important people and pets.
- Help your child have a healthy goodbye.

What You Can Do Right Now

- Pray the chapter prayer over your child.
- Meditate on Psalm 25:5. Ask God to give you wisdom for how you can lovingly educate your child about memorials and saying goodbye.
- Think back to a time in your life when you had to say goodbye to someone special. What did you need from your parents or caring adults during that time? What was the most healing way you said goodbye? Jot down a few notes in child-friendly language that you can share with your child later.
- Create a visual of this statement: "We live by faith and not by fear." Post it in a public place in your home where all family members can see it (like the refrigerator).

Activities You Can Do This Week with Your Child

- As soon as possible, spend at least 15 minutes with your child, carefully attuning to his needs. Ask how his heart is feeling about the great loss. Ask if he wants to do anything special to say goodbye and how you can help him do it.

- Tell your child about times when you said goodbye to someone special. Talk about what helped your heart heal the most. Remind your child that it's goodbye for now, not goodbye forever.
- If your child is ready for it, walk through the healthy goodbye process together to say goodbye to someone special.
- Invite your child to write a letter, draw a picture, or use some other format to express his loss and to say goodbye.

Dear Grandma,

I feel sad that you died. I will miss you at christmas because you always hang our stockings. I hope you like heaven and are dancing a lot.

Love,
Sam

9

Blessed Are Those Who Mourn

Wisdom Principle

Allow your child to mourn.

The LORD is close to the brokenhearted,
and saves those who are crushed in spirit.

PSALM 34:18

An elementary school principal told me a story about three siblings whose parent suddenly died of an unforeseen medical problem. The children saw their parent die because the death occurred in their home. The death happened on a Wednesday, and the funeral was Saturday.

Monday morning, the kids were back on the bus to school.

Why shouldn't the kids be back in school? After all, their other parent probably was returning to work that same day, after the standard two days of bereavement leave. There were bills to pay, and now there was only one income. The funeral was over, and the extended family had returned home. There was no one to provide child care, and besides, what would the kids do at home alone anyway? They seemed okay, and they were probably better off in school, surrounded by their friends. Or were they?

Children need to mourn their great losses. Mourning requires time for one to express deep sorrow over the death or loss of something or someone. It is the way that our hearts, bodies, and minds release grief.

Mourning is a gift from God because its sole purpose is for the grieving individual to receive comfort (Nahum 3:7; Matthew 5:4). "The Lord is close to the brokenhearted and saves those who are crushed in spirit" (Psalm 34:18)—that is, those who are mourning. The desire of God's heart is for grieving children (and parents) to experience his closeness and compassion when their hearts are broken.

Many parents are aware of their grieving child's need to mourn, but they feel inadequate about how to facilitate a mourning season. How much time does a child need to mourn, and what needs to happen? To add to this dilemma, mourning is an uncomfortable topic. It's a tentative thing that is not handled well—or it's ignored altogether. We don't always know what to do or what to say. I'm guessing you might be experiencing some of that tension right now. You need support for our next parenting skill, which is to facilitate a mourning season.

PARENTING SKILL

Facilitate a mourning season.

How to Facilitate a Mourning Season

Begin by making a commitment to *intentionally allow* your child to mourn. The idea of allowing might seem silly, especially if the great loss happened a while ago. But it's not so easy. Many parents have a difficult time recognizing its importance. By allowing, you accept your child's need for a mourning season and her need to include all her thoughts, communication, feelings, and behaviors in this time. Even if your life is now different or harder. Even if you must make major adjustments, like taking some extended time off work. Even if your child's responses trigger your own grief or intense emotions. Even if you didn't like the person or thing your child is grieving. To allow your child to mourn is to stop life as it is—both yours and your child's—in order to attend to your child's needs for comfort and healing.

When you allow your child to mourn, you teach her that mourning is important. Like you, she doesn't know how to mourn. She just feels painful emotions, and she can't see her way through them. By facilitating a mourning season, you give her emotional permission to move through her grief. You teach her that a peaceful, abundant life is a worthy goal and that it is God's intention for her.

Children have special needs during their mourning seasons that are bound by time and activity. A child's mourning season includes four steps—acute mourning, supported mourning, the ceremony, and the new normal.

Acute Mourning

This step is all about comfort, and it lets your child know you are aware of the significance of her great loss. Your job is to attune to your child's feelings as carefully as you can with no other expectations from her. Immediately after the loss, allow your child to refuse to function in any of her life activities. This time can last up to one month, but it could be shorter if your child expresses a desire to move forward. Allow her to stay home from school, family activities, and any other obligations. Make sure your child is always near a loving, supportive adult whom she knows, loves, and trusts. During acute mourning, your child might want to participate in activities she enjoys, such as sports or being with friends. If your child asks to participate in these activities, allow her to do so. This relational connection can be a positive emotional outlet.

Supported Mourning

This step is all about supporting your child's reintegration of her life activities. After two to four weeks of acute mourning, your child will need to go back to some of her normal life activities, such as school. Through supported mourning, you teach your child that she needs to function in some life activities despite her great loss, but you also continue giving her some autonomy over her mourning process. Start by integrating your child back into her required activities and gradually add other activities as she expresses interest in them. Check in often with your child to see how she is doing. Check in with other adults who interact with your child, such as teachers, coaches, children's ministers, and friends' parents.

School attendance usually is not optional, but there are ways to make your child's school life better. Ask your child what she might need to be successful when going back to school. Meet with your child's teacher and school counselor before your child's first day back to school and develop a transition plan. The school may be able to provide a modified schedule, a quiet room for studying, various options for recess, or other resources. Make sure your child's principal and office staff are aware of your child's great loss so that they can facilitate a supportive school climate for your child. You may have to advocate for your child in this process, especially if the school expresses concern about your child's educational progress. Be willing to support your child at home, perhaps sitting with her during study time or helping with homework.

The Ceremony

People can thrive after difficult experiences when they are able to draw positive meaning from them. We create meaning by filtering experiences through our hearts and minds, eventually arriving at conclusions that inform our beliefs and behavior. The process of creating meaning helps us answer such tough questions as "Why?" "What for?" and "What does this mean for my life?" Finding positive meaning leads to peace despite tragedy and loss.

Your child will need to make meaning of her great loss in order to move forward and thrive, not just function. Her meaning-making can be represented in a special event called "the ceremony." This event is most effective if it happens after a time of supported mourning but before the new normal is established. It acknowledges the healing that God has done in your child's life and gives her emotional permission to move forward without guilt and without unhealthy attachment to the loss. She does not have to fear or be sad anymore. She doesn't have to identify with the loss or define herself by it. She is free to grow and become all that God has planned for her to be.

You will know when your child is ready for the ceremony when she expresses a desire to move forward. She might not say she's ready for the ceremony, but she will appear to be functioning well in all the areas of life. The ceremony is an informal yet personal event. Your child should be involved in planning and facilitating the ceremony. (I've listed a few ideas for the ceremony at the end of this chapter.) It should be a sacred time when your child remembers and honors the loss and when friends and family can support your child to move forward.

If the great loss impacted your whole family, I encourage you to have a family ceremony. However, you should wait until all members of the family are ready. Otherwise, it could become another source of grief for those family members who are not emotionally prepared. Support each other as you work toward this family goal together, attuning to feelings and using hopeful language.

The New Normal

This step bolsters hope and teaches your child that forward movement is an important life skill. Grieving children know that life will never be the same again. The term "new normal" acknowledges this but also reminds your child that eventually, she can find a new way. It is a hopeful goal—a goal that allows your child to function again. You can use the term "new normal" with your child; children inherently understand what it means.

> Everything's different since Mommy died. We all miss her every day. I know you especially miss her. We are learning to live a new normal together without Mommy. I know she would want us to be happy, and I know she would be so proud of how well you are doing in your art class.

The new normal does not mean that your child will never again experience grief or sadness about the great loss. Within the new normal, you will find a way to practice remembering, which is a way to acknowledge and honor the loss when your child needs it. (Chapter 10 provides some ideas for remembering.)

Acute Mourning	
Why It's Important	**How to Facilitate It**
It acknowledges to your child that you and other adults are aware of the significance of the great loss; it gives your child permission to grieve.	Immediately after the loss, set aside time when your child does not have to function in any life activities, unless she wants to, for up to one month. Attune to her feelings.
Supported Mourning	
Why It's Important	**How to Facilitate It**
It teaches your child that she needs to function in some life activities despite her great loss while giving her some autonomy over the mourning process.	Support your child's reintegration into required life activities (such as school, church, and family activity) for as long as your child needs it; this will likely be one or two years. Attune to her feelings while setting limits.
The Ceremony	
Why It's Important	**How to Facilitate It**
It honors the great loss while giving your child permission to move forward into the new normal.	Discuss the ceremony with your child and allow her to decide when she's ready for it. Allow her to plan and lead the ceremony if she wishes. Set aside a special time and date when people who are important to your child can be present.
Moving Forward into the New Normal	
Why It's Important	**How to Facilitate It**
It bolsters hope and teaches your child that forward movement is an important life skill.	Model healthy forward movement yourself, giving emotional permission to your child to do the same. Attune to her feelings while using hopeful language. Practice remembering. Be aware that your child may grieve for a long time; there is no time limit to grief.

Blessed Are Those Who Mourn

God understands loss, pain, and grief. But it is not his desire for grieving people to stay in grief. He gave us processes for comfort and mourning. In his famous Sermon on the Mount, Jesus said, "Blessed are those who mourn, for they will be comforted" (Matthew 5:4). Jesus is not saying that those who mourn are blessed because they have lost something or someone. In fact, quite the opposite. Jesus reveals that blessing comes as a result of being comforted. Grieving children need comfort. When someone notices your child's pain and extends comfort, she is blessed. It is important to encourage and allow that comfort from others.

Look again at Matthew 5:4. In this statement, Jesus also was providing a countercultural message that being vulnerable is okay. Facilitating a mourning season for your child is going to create some needs of your own. You may need to take time off work or rearrange your activities. You may worry about needing extra time and resources because it triggers feelings of vulnerability. But asking for help is completely acceptable—and so important. You might consider asking your church or family for financial help to get you through a month or two if you take time off work. Or perhaps you know people who can help with meals, child care, or transportation. During our times of greatest need and vulnerability, we experience true love, community, and support. Let others bless you through their support and comfort.

Jesus reveals that blessing comes as a result of being comforted.

Jesus,

My child longs for comfort. I call on you to bring my child peace through mourning. Please give me the wisdom I need to facilitate this mourning season and the motivation to follow through with it. Thank you for your promise to comfort those who mourn, and I claim that promise. In the name of Jesus, blessed is [child's name], for she/he will be comforted.

Amen.

Q: What if my child resists mourning, or we missed the mourning season?

A: Children respond better to what they see than to what they hear. You don't have to use the words "mourning season." Just facilitate it by modeling and leading throughout the process. If you do this quietly and confidently, your child will follow your leadership. However, if your child is not ready for the new normal after one or two years of supported mourning, it might be time for some professional help. See chapter 14 for more information on working with professional counselors.

If you missed the mourning season, not because of your child's resistance but because that time has come and gone, you can still encourage healing and bring comfort. Children will carry grief until it is released, so it's important to back up and make sure the mourning season happens. First, acknowledge that your child needs to mourn, and intentionally allow it. Make a commitment to facilitate a mourning season until your child is ready to move into the new normal. Even though the period of acute mourning is already over, you might take some time off (a day or two) to stop and remember the loss. Then move forward into supported mourning.

Eventually, plan and facilitate the ceremony with your child and then move forward into the new normal. This process might feel a little awkward given the time lapse or if the great loss has not been talked about in your home. It's okay if it's a little messy. Do it anyway. You may get someone to help, such as a pastor, professional counselor, or trusted friend. The important thing is that your child is allowed to mourn.

Art by Annika, age 9

Steps Toward Healing

Draw Strength from This Chapter

- Grieving children need a designated mourning season.
- There are four steps to mourning: acute mourning, supported mourning, the ceremony, and the new normal.
- You can help your child make positive meaning out of the great loss by facilitating a ceremony.
- Jesus promised that those who mourn will receive comfort.

What You Can Do Right Now

- Pray the chapter prayer over your child.
- Meditate on Psalm 34:18 and Matthew 5:4. What events or circumstances have shown you that the Lord has been close to you and your child? How have you and your child received blessings through this journey?
- Reflect on how you've facilitated your child's mourning season. What has gone well? What can you improve?

Activities You Can Do This Week with Your Child: Ideas for Facilitating the Ceremony

- Have your child write a letter or draw a picture about how the deceased would want her to move forward or how your child plans to move forward.
- Light a candle or visit a special place and share memories or stories.
- Read a story or Scripture to your child about hope and moving forward. Ruth 1:1-18 is a wonderful story about a young woman who loses her husband to death and decides

to move forward in faithfulness with her family. She eventually finds love again and becomes part of the lineage of Jesus Christ. Genesis 37 and 39–50 tells the story of Joseph, a young man who was betrayed and abandoned by his family. He suffered great hardship but faithfully moved forward and eventually became a ruler of a country.

- Share your values around death, loss, or life after death with your child—especially values that have to do with moving forward.
- Visit the gravesite, memorial, or special place. Alternatively, spread ashes of the deceased at a special place. Read a poem or Scripture. Your child can leave a letter, pictures, or other memorabilia there.
- Give your child a special framed photograph of the lost one or thing that she can keep in her room or in a special place.

10

Remembering

Wisdom Principle

Move forward while still remembering the loss.

The memory of the righteous is a blessing.

Proverbs 10:7 esv

It's Kevin's wedding day, a day he's looked forward to his whole life. A handsome 25-year-old college graduate, Kevin has grown into an amazing young man. His bride is the most beautiful woman he's ever met, and they have a bright future ahead of them. He's 100 percent sure about their union, and so is she. But as he looks in the mirror to straighten his tie, a familiar emptiness sinks through his heart. A restless wondering. *Am I going to be a good husband? Am I going to be a good father? What would Dad say if he were here today? Would he be proud of me?*

Kevin's father was killed in the line of duty when Kevin was five years old. He remembers his father vaguely. His mother raised him and his sister, surrounded by a large, supportive extended family. Overall, Kevin feels a peace about his father's death; his family was able to process their grief and move on in a healthy way. His mother remarried, and Kevin has a great relationship with his stepdad. But there are times, like this day, when Kevin's heart feels more vulnerable. He thinks about his dad all the time even though he was so young when his dad died. Unsure of how to put his feelings into words, and not wanting to spoil the day, Kevin puts the finishing touches on his tuxedo and walks through the door to embrace his future.

Grief Is Forever

Grief is different from all other emotions. Grief comes as a direct result of loss, and loss means that the lost person or thing is gone forever. If we were to apply logic, we would assume that if loss is forever, then grief is forever. Yet somehow there is a cultural expectation that grieving children will get over it and move on: "That happened when you were a kid. Your family is happy now, and you have a great future ahead of you. You're not over it yet?" Many, many people, especially those who have not experienced great loss, carry a false logic: If loss is forever, then time should heal it. Get over it and move on.

No. Like all grieving children, Kevin is not over it. He will never get over it. The loss of Kevin's father is permanent. Therefore, Kevin's grief is permanent.

A child's grief never ends. Acute and supported mourning usually subside between six months and two years, but grief continues throughout a child's life. It is triggered afresh by anniversaries and reminders of the loss. Children also experience grief again during their significant life events and developmental stages. Birthdays. Big soccer games. Graduations. Weddings. And especially the birth of their own children. They are keenly aware that someone or something is missing.

Grieving children and families often have a lot of external support during the first year after a loss. This support is necessary and a significant part of healing. But support usually tapers off in the second year and beyond.[1] Other people move on with their lives. They forget, or they assume that the grieving child is no longer grieving because he has seemingly adjusted to his new normal. But your child will always grieve his great loss. The grief may not be all-consuming every day, like it is right after the loss. Instead, it will seem like the grief is sleeping, awakened at certain times in your child's life.

Children also grieve losses of people or things they didn't know well. Kevin was very young when his father died, and he didn't spend a lot of time with his father to begin with. His memories of his father are blurry.

It would be so easy for Kevin's family to assume that Kevin wouldn't grieve his father throughout his life because he didn't know his father, but that assumption would be incorrect. Not only do children grieve the lost person or thing; *they grieve what they missed out on because of the loss*, especially if it was something significant to their development, connection, or identity.

For Kevin, growing up without his biological father meant missing out on father-son fishing trips and other activities his friends got to do with their dads. He missed out on seeing pride on his dad's face when he did something well. He missed out on his father's unique wisdom, as well as the opportunity to know how his father felt about him and the dreams his father had for Kevin's life.

Kevin grieves the loss of something that other people enjoyed but he didn't. And to Kevin, the fact that he didn't get to experience what everyone else did might mean something about him. He might hold a deep fear that he won't be a good father because he didn't know his own father. He's carried a lot of unanswered questions throughout his life, and he'll face new questions at every new developmental step.

Not only do children grieve the lost person or thing; *they grieve what they missed out on because of the loss.*

Kevin might fear that talking about his father at a happy event could ruin a special day—a fear he's felt during most of the happy events of his life. Kevin probably won't speak about his feelings because he might not even be aware of them, or he might not use the word "grief" to describe them. He's just aware of a small, nagging feeling, a hole in his heart, or a knot in his stomach. He doesn't slow down to address any of this. He's learned to just straighten out his tie and move on.

Grieving children don't know how to address their grief; they are rarely taught how to do so. Other people overlook grief, and that's one of the reasons grieving children feel so alone. Your child isn't sure whether he is supposed to grieve, whether he is even grieving, or how to talk about it. His difficulty is compounded if no one else seems to recognize his feelings.

Imagine how Kevin would feel today if he heard this: "You have a great future ahead of you. You have a great stepdad who's going to stand up with you today. Why are you thinking about something that happened when you were five years old? Let's be happy and celebrate today!" That kind of statement would only deepen the hole in his heart. Instead, Kevin needs wise, caring adults who see and fill up his empty heart with good things before he shows any sign of need. This is critical if Kevin is to process his grief *in this moment*, which is but one small step in his journey toward healing.

Remember with Mementos

One of my most treasured possessions is my grandmother's recipe box. I was the lucky granddaughter in the family who got it after she died. All her recipes are there in her own handwriting. Some even have stains of the food she made when she was using them! When I miss my grandma, I can pull out her recipe box, find a well-worn recipe (a sign of the ones she loved the most), and make it.

My grandmother's recipe box was something she used every day, and just seeing it takes me right back to my eight-year-old self trying to find where she hid the freshly baked chocolate chip cookies in her small kitchen. If I close my eyes, I can smell the cookies and hear the rattling lid of the Dutch oven where she always kept them. And she's right there with me, chuckling and enjoying the whole scene. The experience is bittersweet because my brain knows she's not really there, but my heart fully feels her and connects with her.

It's the heart that must heal in grief, not the head. People can logically understand death and loss; even very young children can understand it. But from the heart, we experience love and attachment, connection and relationship, which are the real losses after great loss. Mementos like my grandma's recipe box are powerful sensory reminders, and they reconnect your child with his lost loved one. They also remind your child that the loved one is never really gone. Mementos are tangible pieces of that person that your child can interact with at any time.

If it is possible, display mementos of the lost person or thing. Photographs or memory boxes are wonderful ways to display them. Even better, use them if they are stable and practical for everyday use. It may be painful to have a daily reminder of the loss, but with the pain also comes permission for your child to feel what he feels and to reconnect with the loved one. If it is possible, find personal items of the deceased loved one. Share or show these items to your child and put them in a place where your child can see them. If possible, let your child use them or play with them. Talk about them. How did your child's loved one get that jacket or trophy, knickknack, tool, or piece of jewelry? Why was it special or useful? If your child is old enough, give him one or more of these mementos or keep them in a safe place until he can be responsible for them.

If your child's great loss was his family through divorce or being removed from his home and put into the foster care system, it might be awkward or inappropriate to have mementos or photos of the former family in the public spaces in your home. But do allow your child to have mementos of his first family in his own personal spaces, like his room. These mementos could include wedding photos of his parents, family photos, and other special things. In fact, don't just allow this—facilitate it! Your child is unlikely to ask for mementos, especially if there has been a lot of family conflict. He may not even know the mementos exist. A child's first family is where he came from, and recognizing and honoring these mementos gives a very clear message to your child that you recognize and honor him.

Remember It to Move On

One of your most important assignments is to facilitate remembering for your grieving child. You might fear that reminding your child of the great loss will do more harm than good. After all, won't remembering it just bring up your child's pain afresh? But it's critical to understand that *remembering is not reminding*. Remembering is an intentional pause to acknowledge your child's loss and give your child permission to feel any feelings he has about the loss in that moment.

It is an inclusion of someone or something that should be there but is missing.

Remembering is a critical part of healing because it honors a part of your child that is tangibly gone but ever present in his heart. For grieving children, remembering great loss is not just honoring a person or thing. It's also giving your child the chance to experience what he missed out on. For all children, this experience is critical to healthy development and proper formation of identity, and to learning how to have healthy connection through relationship.

> Remembering is not reminding. Remembering gives your child permission to feel any feelings he has about the loss in that moment.

Remembering your child's great loss might seem counterintuitive to you. We adults have already accomplished these critical developmental tasks and might not immediately understand how remembering a great loss would help facilitate healthy development. But when you intentionally model remembering and facilitate it with your child, you give your child permission to remember and include the lost person or thing in any situation throughout his life.

We arrive now at our next parenting skill, which is to move forward while still remembering the loss. In a paradoxical way, remembering is a healthy part of moving forward.

PARENTING SKILL

Move forward while still remembering the loss.

As I write this chapter, again I am prompted by the Holy Spirit to think of how you yourself may be experiencing deep pain and grief. My suggestion that you facilitate a mourning and remembering process might be difficult for you to even conceptualize. It might trigger a guilt reaction: *I can't*, or *I'm a bad parent if I don't do this*. Be encouraged—you don't need to do it perfectly, because there is no perfect way to do it. Remembering doesn't have to be a big, overwhelming, planned-out thing. It can be simple—a brief comment or sentiment, a photograph, or a shared memento. (I've included a few more ideas at the end of this chapter.) You don't have to do it now, especially if you can't. This might be a great time to reach out to your support system and elicit their help.

But I invite you to at least be open to the idea of remembering. If you are grieving too, remembering can be an important part of your own journey toward healing. Remembering a great loss together can be a way of building and strengthening your relationship with your child. Just make sure the remembering process is about attuning to your child's needs, and get your own outside support if you need it. The Holy Spirit will give you the strength to do this and the wisdom to know how (John 14:26). He will give you the words to say and ideas for unique and special activities just for your child to help him remember his loved one.

Kevin's wedding day would be complete with a connection with his father, even a very small one. How it would fill his heart for his mother to comment, "You look so much like your dad today! My heart is brimming with love and joy for you, and I know your dad's heart is overflowing with love and joy for you too." How freeing would it be for Kevin's stepdad to say, "I am so glad I got to raise you, and I honor the man who gave you life. Without him, I would not have gotten the gift of a son and a new daughter-in-law." What favor it would be for Kevin's grandmother to give him the same kiss on the forehead and blessing she gave his father on his wedding day. What a gift indeed it would be for Kevin's grandfather to give Kevin a pocket watch, the same gift he gave Kevin's father when he came of age. What a release for everyone at the wedding—both families—to know they have permission to acknowledge all of Kevin's history while celebrating their great joy for the future.

When you help your child remember the past, you release him to move forward into his future. You free your child to understand, allow, and process his emotions. Children cannot get over it and move on. Rather, they remember it and move on.

Jesus,

I long for you to heal my child's grief. You have given us a new normal, but I know that my child's grief is a lifelong journey. I invite you to walk with me and my child as I help him remember his loss in a healing way. Give me the wisdom to recognize his need to remember and process the great loss, especially during significant life events. Give me the words to say and ideas for activities or mementos that will aid in his remembering. I ask you to always be present with my child so that he feels your presence as he moves forward into the amazing future you have planned for him.

Amen.

Q: What if I've missed the chance to facilitate remembering?

A: If you are reading this book years after your child's great loss, you might fear that it's too late for remembering. Bringing up death, loss, or a deceased loved one is incredibly difficult, and parents often are unsure how to facilitate remembering. But it's never too late. Even if your child is now an adult, you can start remembering today. I guarantee that your child still remembers his great loss, and your intentional remembering will be very healing for him. Read through the suggestions at the end of this chapter and pray for wisdom from the Holy Spirit to help your child remember. Pick one or more of the activities below and ask your child if he would be willing to remember with you.

Steps Toward Healing

Draw Strength from This Chapter

- Children experience grief throughout their lives, especially during important life events and key developmental stages.
- Mementos of the lost person or thing help facilitate remembering and healing.
- Parents are instrumental in facilitating their child's remembering process.

What You Can Do Right Now

- Pray the chapter prayer over your child.
- Meditate on Proverbs 10:7a and John 14:26. What has God taught you about grief and your child's needs? What are some ways you can help him remember?
- Think about your own great losses. How have you remembered them? What did you need from others to help you remember? Jot down a few notes.
- Mark the date of your child's great loss (and any other significant events about the great loss, such as the deceased person's birthday) on the calendar. Do a remembering activity with your child on these dates every year.

Activities You Can Do This Week with Your Child

- Write out some of your memories of your child's deceased loved one or lost thing (such as a former community or a pet). Describe some events that give your child an accurate picture of his loved one. Read these memories out loud to your child, or save them for a scrapbook or collage.

- Create a collage or scrapbook of the loved one and your child. Allow your child to keep these items in his room or in a special place.
- Include the deceased loved one in some way at every one of your child's special events (graduation, wedding, and so on). Even a very simple verbal acknowledgment is powerful.

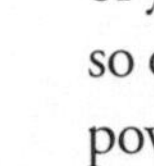

- Cook the loved one's favorite food. Go to the grocery store with your child and allow him to select the ingredients. Make the meal together. Play the loved one's favorite songs while you are cooking. Eat the meal together and tell funny stories about your child's loved one.
- Select one of the loved one's favorite games and play it with your child. Tell him why his loved one enjoyed the game.
- Remember the deceased loved one on their birthday and the anniversary of their death. Ask your child how he would like to facilitate the remembrance.
- Create or purchase a special Christmas ornament that remembers and honors the great loss. Or find an ornament that belonged to the loved one. During the holidays, decorate the Christmas tree or your child's stocking with this ornament. Talk about special holiday memories with the loved one.

Art by Annika, age 9

11

The Loss of a Parent

Wisdom Principle

Children are forever attached to their parents, even if their parents are not present.

A father to the fatherless, a defender of widows, is God in his holy dwelling.

Psalm 68:5

Jesse's father got cancer when she was ten years old. His death was devastating to Jesse and her mother. Their community provided comfort and support, but things were different for Jesse from that point on. Now an adult, she reflects on how her friends and community reacted after her father's death: "For the most part, I was treated normally. But there was a sense, a small feeling, that I was now different from all my peers. It was a lonely place to be."

Millions of children in the United States and worldwide experience the loneliness that Jesse felt. In the United States alone, one in every 20 children will experience the death of a parent by the age of 15.[1] Foster children represent the majority of US children who have lost a parent; by the age of 18, one in eight foster children have experienced the death of at least one parent.[2] Each day, 120,000 children are living with widowed fathers in the United States.[3] Millions more children lose relationships with their parents every year due to divorce or abandonment.

Every day, these grieving children walk among us with broken hearts, trying to fit in as best as they can. They are treated just like any other kid. But therein lies the problem: *They are not just any other kid.* They are kids who feel lost and alone, trying not to rock the boat or draw attention to themselves. They are trying their best to survive in a world where the unthinkable can happen...and sometimes does. It happened to them.

The loss of a parent is the single biggest developmental trauma a child can face. On a practical level, loss of a parent creates a significant amount of upheaval in a child's day-to-day life because she has lost a primary caregiver. Financial challenges often follow the death of a parent, sometimes to the extent that the child must survive in poverty. Sometimes the family must relocate, which means not only reestablishing community but also going to a new school and forming a new peer group. Sometimes relocating means moving in with extended family with different rules and expectations—another major adjustment. Children who have lost a parent almost always live in single-parent households for a while. If the surviving parent recouples, these children are again faced with significant childhood stressors—stepparent and blended-family issues.

Grieving children walk among us with broken hearts, trying to fit in as best as they can.

But the greatest loss these children experience is a loss of part of themselves.[4] When a parent dies or is absent, half of the child's identity goes with that parent. This loss of self significantly challenges the child's identity formation, especially in children who lose a parent early in childhood. God's perfect design was for children to have two unique parents. Both parents significantly contribute to the child's understanding of who she is and where she came from. The loss of self through the loss of a parent complicates the child mourner's task. She's not just mourning the loss of a person she loved. She must now renegotiate life after losing a piece of her identity. She must learn who she is and find her unique place in the world without her teacher—a teacher who loved her unconditionally.

All at the ripe old age of ten.

I Know Where My Dad Is

> I can't stand the phrase, "I'm sorry for your loss." I remember thinking, *I haven't lost my dad. I know where he is. His body is in the ground.* —Jesse

There is one key difference between the way children process the death or loss of a parent and the way adults process it: Children have an ongoing relationship with their dead or absent parent.[5] Children understand they won't see their parent again, but they continue to share a bond as if the parent were still present. In the child's mind, the parent still exists. Your child will continue to talk to her parent, think about her parent, and include her parent in all aspects of her life. Her missing parent is always still there.

This ongoing bond might seem strange to you as an adult, but it actually becomes clearer when we consider a child's normal developmental task of identity formation. By remaining connected with the deceased parent, your child has a sense that she still belongs to someone. She is a person who came from a person; she has a name and a purpose. This ongoing bond not only brings her comfort in her great loss but also forms the foundation for her to discover who she is and who she will become.

Understanding this concept is so very critical because you, now the primary caregiver for your child, must facilitate this ongoing parent-child relationship. We've arrived at our next parenting skill, which is to help children who have lost a parent facilitate an ongoing bond with that parent.

PARENTING SKILL

Help children who have lost a parent
facilitate an ongoing bond with that parent.

This concept might feel ambiguous. Take some time to let it sink in. How do you facilitate a relationship between a child and a person who isn't there? This might seem awkward, strange...perhaps even a little delusional. But for your child, it is a critical step toward healing because it acknowledges her mourning process and helps her establish her unique identity and sense of self-esteem.

Acknowledge and allow the parent-child relationship.

Though your child has an ongoing relationship with her missing parent, it is unlikely that she will ever speak about it out loud. The bond is more emotional than cognitive, which means the child *feels* it rather than thinks about it. Verbal communication is processed through the brain rather than the heart, and therefore your child may not speak about her feelings spontaneously. She will need a little help. You can provide a safe place for your child to express her feelings. Ask her how she feels about her missing parent and use language that suggests that your child still has a relationship with her parent. If your child is very young, provide opportunities for expression through art, music, or play.

Unless they are asked, children might not speak about their ongoing relationship with the missing parent because they know other people don't understand it. Or they may feel that others don't want to listen. That's how Jesse felt: "Later in high school, I sometimes mentioned my dad's death in a conversation or a classroom discussion. One of my peers said, 'Get over it...it happened years ago.'" When children don't feel safe, seen, heard, or understood, they are silent. They need a caring adult—especially a caregiver or parent—to acknowledge their feelings exactly where they are, allow them to feel them, and give them permission to express them in any way the children need to.

Actively facilitate the relationship through intentional and positive connection with the missing parent.

Your child may never talk about her deceased parent, and she may shrug off reminders of her parent. She may respond blankly when someone mentions her parent. This response is normal; many children grieve by not responding. Like Jesse, grieving children tend to adapt because that's what they've been taught to do. If a child is going to adapt, then let her follow a healthy model of how to be in an ongoing relationship with the deceased parent. Your child needs you to be the role model for this process.

Provide opportunities for your child to connect with her missing parent. Include the missing parent during special events in your child's life. If your child appears reticent, do it gently: "You look so much like your mom in that dress...I know she's smiling down on you today," or "Your dad was really good at football, just like you." Simple comments like these go a long way. If your child seems open to this, try lighting a candle and placing a photo of the missing parent on a decorated table for your child's birthday celebration. Consider giving your child a personal item of the parent as a memento during a rite of passage.

Provide tangible, physical reminders of the parent.

Children who have lost a parent benefit from mementos and memories of that parent, but they benefit even more from tangible reminders. Electronic video and audio recordings have the most impact because your child can hear her parent's voice and see their body language. Recordings are precious reminders of the missing parent's voice, the parent's sense of humor, and special times spent together. Other tangible evidence includes letters, stories, poems, work projects, journals, or other documents written in the parent's handwriting. Help your child see how her parent helped form her history.

When a Parent Is Dying

A child who is facing the pending loss of a parent because of a terminal illness faces some extra challenges. The process leading up to the parent's death is stressful for the entire family, and the child's needs are often overlooked. Children can be misinformed about their parent's health status and show signs of stress rather than grief (see chapter 3). Children react to their parents' terminal illnesses in different ways. They may refuse to see the parent or cling to the parent or other adults. These children are often afraid they will get sick and die too. All these reactions are very normal.

Sometimes adults are too optimistic or afraid of worrying the child, so they minimize the status of the illness. Sometimes adults are in denial because of their own grief. And sometimes adults themselves do not know the severity of a loved one's health status. Always be honest with children about their parents' illnesses and possible deaths. Children can be so misinformed about their parent's terminal health status that the death takes them by surprise. In Jesse's case, this surprise added an extra layer to her grief: "That was probably the hardest part...I never felt like he was going to die until it actually happened."

A terminally ill parent's energy levels, mood, and even personality may change drastically. They may exhibit interactions that are shocking or difficult for your child to process. This is especially challenging, so be aware that your child may feel she has lost her parent even before the death.

Talking with your child about all these possibilities is important. Help her realize her feelings and reactions are normal. Lovingly validate your child's feelings even if she does not want to interact with the terminally ill parent. If you feel your child should have some final interactions with the terminal parent, do what you can to encourage and support your child through the visits. The communication model in chapter 4 will help you talk to children about a parent's terminal health status. It can be used by any adult, but it is best if both parents sit down with the child together and communicate through each step.

Always be honest with children about their parents' illnesses and possible deaths.

Terminally ill parents can bring comfort to their children and ease the grieving process significantly. Understanding that their deaths will impact their children's identity formation, terminally ill parents can make steps to confirm the parent-child relationship and the child's identity. Here are some beautiful ways to confirm the child's identity: Share stories of how the child came to be—about your life, how you met your child's other parent, and how you decided to have children.

Tell your child how you chose her name, and share some of the hopes and dreams you have for her life. If possible, record these conversations so your child can have them for the rest of her life.

These final moments together can be powerful. They release the child to grieve the death of a parent, and they encourage the child to move toward healing. Consider having the dying parent give your child a blessing before their death. In the Bible, a parent blessed a child as a sign of God's favor for the rest of the child's life. It occurred during a rite of passage or prior to a parent's death. A blessing is a spiritual symbol of attachment and favor from the parent and from God. The blessing should be written out so the child can keep it forever, but the parent should also speak it over the child. There is no right way to give a blessing, but consider including these elements:

- the child's full name and the meaning of the name
- the parent's unending love for the child
- the parent's hopes and dreams for the child's future, including some character qualities the parent desires the child to have
- a request for God's blessing and favor over the child
- a reminder that the parent will forever be with the child, even in death

Forever Attached

In chapter 5, you learned that attachment is your child's ability to bond and form close relationships. Not only is attachment validated by science; it also is a spiritual principle. God created attachment so children can develop into whole, complete adults who can establish and maintain healthy relationships. Attachment develops from the parent-child relationship early in life. And attachment to the parent never ends, even when it is interrupted by death or absence.

Your child will be forever attached to her deceased or absent parent. Forever attached. Help your child discover her unique identity by knowing who and where she came from. Though that parent is now missing from her day-to-day life, you can validate that attachment by using the simple suggestions in this chapter to honor the missing parent.

Help your child discover her unique identity by knowing who and where she came from.

God created attachment, and he understands the longing of a child's heart to know and have relationship with her parents. And because he created attachment, he is attached to us. Psalm 68:5 says, "A father to the fatherless, a defender of widows, is God in his holy dwelling." God is a forever parent to all children, including you. He is forever attached to your child, and he's forever attached to you.

If you are the parent with the illness or you are now the widowed parent, find comfort in knowing that God sees both your pain and your child's pain. You and your child are significant to him. He promises to fill in the gap where you and your child need it the most. Nurturing. Comfort. Provision. Protection. Identity formation. Jesus has got it covered. Take a moment right now to ask God to provide these things for your child and your family.

Jesus,

My child yearns for [father/mother]. I wish I could provide all the love and attachment she needs, but I can't. Only you can, Jesus. You promise in Psalm 68:5 that you are a forever parent to every child. I ask you to move toward my child right now and meet her need for [father/mother]. I ask you to move toward me right now and meet my need for a provider and helper. Help us move forward while still having a connection to our loved one. I feel your compassion and love right now, Jesus. Help my child feel it too.

Amen.

Q: What if my child didn't get her blessing?

A: The Bible tells the story of a son (Esau) who missed out on his rightful blessing from his father (Genesis 27). However, we see later in Esau's story that God blessed Esau so much that he had everything he needed (Genesis 32:3-21; 33:9). Parents love their children even after death; their love provides a spiritual connection that supersedes death. Thus a child doesn't actually "miss out on" a blessing from a parent. If a formal blessing did not occur prior to the parent's death, you can still tell your child how the deceased or absent parent would have wished to bless her. Take a few moments to review the bullet points above about how to give a parent-child blessing. Consider how the absent parent would have responded to these points and then write out these responses. You can add some personal thoughts as well so the blessing comes from both of you. At a special time, share this blessing with your child.

Steps Toward Healing

Draw Strength from This Chapter

- Loss of identity is the greatest loss for children who have lost parents.
- The surviving parent facilitates an ongoing bond between the child and deceased or absent parent.
- Terminally ill parents can bring comfort to their children by being honest about their health status, confirming the parent-child relationship, and establishing their children's identities through a blessing.

What You Can Do Right Now

- Pray the chapter prayer over your child.
- Meditate on Psalm 68:5. Write out what that verse means to you right now. Write out how this verse is special to your child right now.
- Look up the meaning of your child's name—in particular, its biblical meaning, if it has one. In the Bible, naming a child was a spiritual practice that designated new life, a connection to the family line, and the child's life purpose. God gave the privilege of naming a child to the child's parents. If you don't know already, find out how your child got her name and what role the other parent had in naming your child.
- Look up the meaning and cultural heritage of your child's last name and write down a few fun facts to share with your child later. These insights will help your child to form her identity.

Activities You Can Do This Week with Your Child

- Read Psalm 68:5 out loud to your child. Talk about how God is a forever parent who will never leave her. Share with your child what that verse means to you and ask what it means to her.
- Share with your child what you learned about her name, the role the other parent had in choosing it, and its cultural heritage. If your child is young, draw a picture about this together. Ask your child to include the missing parent in the picture.
- Find a way to reconnect your child with the missing parent. (See some of the suggestions earlier in the chapter.)
- Go to a special place that the missing parent loved. Did that parent have a favorite park, river, or activity? Or go to the place where your child's parent was born, grew up, went to school, or visited. Tell your child about her parent's connection to that place.

Dear Mom, I really miss you.
Did you Know I made the baseball
team this year? And I got an A in
math. I wish you were here to help
me with math because I hate it. But
I Know that you are good at math
and Want me to do well. So I try really
hard. Dad says that you sing with
the angels every night. Talk to you soon.
Love, Micah

Art by Micah, age 9

12

The Death or Disability of a Sibling

Wisdom Principle

Every child in your family needs their own identity and purpose.

God sets the lonely in families,
he leads out the prisoners with singing.

Psalm 68:6

How are your parents doing?"

It's the never-ending question for children who have lost a sibling to death or disability. And oh, do they ever understand why they are asked that question. They watched their parents—and sometimes they watched their sibling—walk through hell on earth. Hospitals. Doctors. Medical bills piled up on the dining room table. Hushed voices intermingled with sobs of pain. These children know the immense burden their parents are carrying, all the while wishing and wanting to help but not knowing how.

Children who have lost a sibling have a triple loss. They lose their sibling and everything that means for their childhood…their first peer relationship, camaraderie, and shared family experiences. They lose the attention of their parents. And they lose their family unit as they have known it. These are the grieving children who are overlooked most often. There is so much going on, and they don't want to create any more stress. Everyone else has bigger problems to solve than theirs, so they fade into the shadows, unseen.

If It's All You Can Do, It's Enough

Dearest parent, this chapter fills my heart with heaviness. If your child has lost a sibling, then you or someone very close to you has lost a child. Losing a child is the biggest tragedy anyone can experience. If this is you, I want to take a moment to pause and recognize your deep pain. Your emptiness. Your sorrow. Your shock, your disbelief. The reorganization in your entire psyche of everything that is supposed to be good and true and right. Guilt, as if wanting and wishing to create a human life out of love and for love could be selfish. Barely getting through each day. Not being able to take care of your own needs, let alone someone else's.

You are deeply concerned for your grieving child—otherwise you would not be reading this book. Your heart's desire is to love your child, parent him, meet his needs. Your heart breaks again every time you see your child feeling lonely and overlooked. But you are likely overwhelmed by your own grief, which makes it hard to care for him right now.

I understand this, and everyone else does too. Even your grieving child understands it.

Here are a few simple things to know and do for your grieving child. If this is all you can do right now, remember...it's enough.

Your child will feel a lifelong bond with his sibling.

Just as children who have lost a parent have a lifelong relationship with that parent, children who have lost a sibling have a lifelong bond with that sibling.[1] Children form their identity by being a part of a family, and siblings are part of that identity. Your child knows that his family is incomplete because someone is missing—his brother or sister. Because of this absence, your child will want to include his sibling throughout his life in special ways.

It might feel easier to try to push down your feelings about the loss of a child, to grieve and try to move on. Besides, people outside of the family don't always recognize the significance of the loss of a child, especially in the case of a miscarriage or neonatal death. But you know that another child (or more than one) is part of your family. So does your child. You can help your child by remembering his sibling. (See chapter 10 for some ideas.) Help your child realize the sibling bond lasts a lifetime, and support your child's efforts to include and remember the sibling. Your child may need to process several times at different points in his life what the death of a sibling means. His personal meaning about the loss may change over time.

Your child feels a sense of survivor guilt.

Your child might feel as if he's done something wrong because he survived when his sibling didn't or because he is healthy when his sibling wasn't. Of course, this feeling is not rational, and you would never want your child to feel this way. Survivor guilt is a reaction to a trauma. It comes from a desire and willingness to bear the pain of another—but not being able to. Your child needs to hear that neither he nor anyone else is responsible for what happened to his sibling. He could not have stopped it no matter how much he wanted to or how hard he prayed.

You can help your child by helping him understand he is not responsible for the loss of his sibling, and he is not responsible for comforting you in your grief: "We are all so sad your baby sister died, and we'll be sad for a long time. It's hard to understand why sad things like this happen sometimes, and we will trust Jesus to give us the answers. You need to know that there was nothing you could have done to stop her from dying. And you're not responsible for taking care of me. My job is to take care of you even though I'm sad."

Your child wonders if he's enough for you.

Your child's heart is in a conflicted place. On one hand, he feels his own deep loss as well as sadness about your loss. On the other hand, he wonders why you are so sad even though you still have him. If you decide to have another child after your loss, his feelings might compound even more. Again, these feelings are not rational...but feelings are never rational to begin with!

Help your child understand that your desire for more children is not to replace him or his sibling but rather to create more love in your family: "We love you so much, and we will always love and remember your baby sister in heaven. No one will ever replace you or her. We want to create more love in our family, which is why we are having another baby. We love you so much, and we're so glad you are our son. Our family would not be complete without you."

Your child will renegotiate his place in the family.

One of the reasons God established family is so that children can find their place in the world. Children have different roles and responsibilities in the family depending on their birth order. When a family loses a child, the roles and responsibilities in the family shift. For example, your child might transition from being the oldest child to an only child—with new expectations. This shifting of roles and responsibilities might be unintentional, but it likely will happen. As a result, your child will go through a process of rediscovering who he is, including his contribution to his family and place within it.

You can help your child by reminding him of his special and important place in your family. Talk with him about how it feels for the sibling birth order to be different and help him identify the changes that has brought for him. Intentionally look for things he's good at outside his role in the family and affirm them out loud. Help him find significance through relationships and activities that help establish his identity. This significance will lead to feelings of connection and purpose.

PARENTING SKILL

Help children who have lost a sibling feel connected and purposeful.

This parenting skill is the most powerful thing you can do for your child. Connection and purpose create a hopeful path to healing a displaced heart. Take a few moments to reflect on these principles and how you might apply them with your child. And remember again, dear parent, if this is all you can do right now...it's enough.

Loss of a Sibling Who Is Still Alive

Children may lose siblings not to death but rather to difficult circumstances, such as special needs, divorce, or foster care. Children experiencing the loss of a sibling in this manner may never express their needs or challenges around their loss...or even acknowledge that it is indeed a loss. Moreover, adults can easily overlook these sibling losses because of the multiple and complex stressors the parents also are facing.

Siblings with Special Needs

Children who have living siblings with special needs experience loss. Even though the sibling is alive, your child (and family) experiences the loss of what could have been had that child not had special needs. This type of loss is one of the most difficult because people often don't talk about it or even acknowledge it. Your child may not talk about it either—he loves you and his sibling, so he may feel guilty about expressing his loss. Your child needs permission to mourn what he missed out on. He needs permission to feel anything he's feeling about the needs of his sibling, including embarrassment or frustration. He needs permission to just be a kid without taking on the responsibilities of adults.

And he needs a relationship with his sibling. Despite the challenges he may face, your child deeply loves and feels an unbreakable bond with his brother or sister. Children who grow up with a sibling with special needs often develop empathy, protectiveness, and responsibility. These are wonderful traits to have. Affirm them and celebrate them in your child. At the same time, recognize that your child should not be taking adults' responsibilities while he's still a child. Encourage your child to display these positive traits only to further the sibling bond and not to take on the parents' responsibilities.

Family Changes

A child who loses a sibling through family changes, such as divorce or foster care, experiences the same losses—his place in the family, an attachment, camaraderie, and a relationship. The sisterhood has been divorced; the brotherhood has been broken. If adults are engaged in hostile or difficult interactions with other family members, they may fail to see how a major family transition might impact the sibling relationships (even with stepsiblings). Think about how awkward it would be for a child to refer to "my old brother whose dad was my first stepfather."

With a change in family relationships, children aren't always allowed to maintain sibling relationships, especially if they are very young. Parents can help their children by encouraging them to maintain sibling relationships despite the family change. Allow your child to continue to address the former sibling as "brother" or "sister" if he wishes. Ensure that your child sees his sibling in a positive and encouraging environment and context rather than a hostile one.

Identity and Purpose

Every child in your family needs his own identity and purpose. As you've read this chapter, I imagine that helping your child form his own special identity and purpose might seem overwhelming. But it's actually simple. One of the easiest and best ways to form your child's unique identity and purpose is to speak affirmations to him. Here are some simple affirmations to remind your child of his precious worth:

- "You are loved."
- "You have a special place in this family."
- "You are such a good brother/sister."
- "You have permission to love all your family members—past, present, future, living with us, or living in our hearts."
- "You have special gifts to use inside and outside of this family." (Name a few of those gifts you see.)

You created your children out of love and for love, and that's the way God created us. That love gives us connection and purpose. God doesn't want us to be lonely or displaced; that's why he's given us families (Psalm 68:6). Try to make your family the foundational place where your child finds love, connection, and purpose.

Jesus,

My child's heart is displaced and hurting. He has missed out on a special sibling bond, and his heart is heavy. I invite you to fill the lonely places, Jesus. Help him understand that he doesn't have to carry this burden. Help me see my child's needs and attune to them even though I am overwhelmed and brokenhearted too. Please meet us at this incredibly difficult part of our family's journey, Jesus. We trust you to make something beautiful out of our pain.

Amen.

Q: How do we answer the question, "How many children/siblings do you have?"

A: This question is like a punch to the gut for families that have lost a child. The answer to this question is something that you should discuss and agree upon as a family. This will be a hard conversation, no doubt. But having the conversation is important for a couple of reasons. First, it is an opportunity to process and mourn your loss together. Second, it helps your child know exactly what to say and exactly what you are going to say, thus reducing awkwardness and pain. Preparing for this difficult question will help your child navigate future life situations.

There is no right answer to this question; the right answer is what you decide on as a family. Your child may choose to share the number of living siblings, or he may choose to share that his brother or sister passed away. Or he may choose different answers for different contexts. Help him choose an answer that brings him the most peace.

- "I have one sister who lives with me and one brother who lives in my heart."
- "I have an older brother. My younger sister passed away six months ago."
- "It's complicated."

Steps Toward Healing

Draw Strength from This Chapter

- Children who lose a sibling often feel out of place and overlooked.
- Connection and purpose can help your child renegotiate his place in the family.
- Children who have lost living siblings need permission to mourn and/or to maintain a relationship with their siblings in their own special ways.

What You Can Do Right Now

- Pray the chapter prayer over your child.
- Think about a time when you felt out of place. What did you need? Jot down a few notes.
- Meditate on the first line of Psalm 68:6. What is God telling you about how to meet the needs of your grieving child?
- Consider calling the school counselor to see if your child can be placed in a special therapeutic group at school. This kind of group will help connect your child with peers who might be going through similar experiences.

Activities You Can Do This Week with Your Child

- Find family photos with all your family members or with just your children together. Help your child create a special picture frame. Many craft stores have frames that can be artfully designed. If you have a limited budget, go to a thrift store and find an old frame. A glue gun and some paint can do wonders! Find small items around the house to glue onto the frame—Scrabble or other game pieces, puzzle pieces, buttons, costume jewelry, or small items that might have belonged to the sibling are all great decorative items. Place the photo in the frame and let your child keep the photo in his bedroom.

- Help your child trace his hand on a piece of paper. For every finger, have your child draw or write something great about himself or something he likes about his life. This process will help your child see that he is important, he is unique, and he has great qualities.
- Designate a "stress-free family chillax" each week where the kids just get to be kids (and you get to take a break from your worries), especially if you have a child with special needs. Play a game, play dress-up, sing a song, or watch a movie. Take lots of photos or videos...eat junk food...and laugh a lot!

Art by Leona, age 10

13

The Loss of a Family

Wisdom Principle

Children who have lost a family need stability.

We have this hope as an anchor for the soul, firm and secure.

HEBREWS 6:19

Jada is a beautiful, curly-haired, healthy little girl. She loves to laugh and play and sneak plums out of the fruit bowl her foster mother keeps on the dining room table—when her foster mom isn't looking, of course. Jada is almost four years old, so she spends most of her day at home or running errands with her foster mom. Occasionally she has a playdate with her half siblings, and she goes to her Cubbies class every Sunday when the family goes to church.

Jada became a foster child when her birth mother took her to a safe house because she could not care for Jada. No questions were asked, so there wasn't a lot of history about Jada's prenatal care and first weeks of life. Soon after, child welfare services got involved and attempted to reunify Jada with her birth parents. The attempts were unsuccessful. Jada's birth mother couldn't kick her drug habit and eventually relinquished her parental rights. Jada's birth father was convicted of drug crimes and sent to prison. He refused to give up his parental rights, so Jada waits in foster care for the next step of her journey. It's not a bad life for Jada. She's been placed with the same family since infancy, and they are mostly all she's ever known. She loves them, and they love her.

A Strong Anchor

You might be parenting a foster child like Jada right now. Or perhaps you are an adoptive parent, or you are a single parent, having recently gone through a divorce. You could be a stepparent of a child who comes and goes from your home. Or you could be a spiritual parent who loves and cares for a child who is not legally yours but is part of your family nonetheless. Part of you feels secure in what you are providing for your child...but part of you wonders if you are providing enough.

Is Jada a grieving child? On the outside, no. She's happy. Her attachment is intact, and she appears to be physically and developmentally on track. But Jada is slowly becoming aware that she is different from other kids. She calls her foster mom Mommy, but she knows her foster mom is not her mommy. She can vaguely remember her birth parents from their supervised visits, and she wonders why her half siblings (the children of her father with another woman) get to live with their "real" mother. Even though she's still so young, Jada wonders why she is different. Why doesn't she live with her parents? Did they not love her enough? Will she ever get to grow up with full biological brothers and sisters? Is she going to get a forever family like other kids?

People assume wrongly that children grieve only when they experience the death of a loved one. But as we have seen, children grieve any great loss. Loss of a family impacts more children in the United States than all other losses combined. The US Census Bureau counted 79.6 million children in the United States in 2016, and that number is growing by the year. Almost 40 million of these children will eventually experience the divorce of their parents and subsequent loss of their first family.

Single-parent families are becoming more common. Twenty-three percent of children live solely with their mothers (almost 17 million children); 4 percent live solely with their fathers (almost 3 million children); and another 4 percent of children do not live with either parent.[1] Seventy-five percent of children from divorced families will live solely with their mothers, losing the daily presence of and relationship with their fathers. At least 11 percent of children from divorced families (4.3 million kids) will become partially or fully alienated from one of their parents and that parent's extended family.[2] Nearly half a million children in the United States live in foster care, and these numbers rise every year. Approximately 25 percent of those foster children are in state custody for more than two years, and many of them live in foster care for most of their childhood.[3]

Children lose their families every single day in the United States. Loss of family is an epidemic.

Loss of a family impacts more children in the United States than all other losses combined.

People are wired for family. God designed us to live in family systems with parents, siblings, grandparents, aunts and uncles, cousins...even cats, dogs, ferrets, and the like! Loss of stability is the greatest loss in the loss of a family. When children lose that stability, they crave it and seek it for the rest of their lives. Our journey has brought us to our next parenting skill, which is to provide stability to children who have lost a family.

PARENTING SKILL

Provide stability to children who have lost a family.

Because the longing for family is hardwired into our brains, children will seek and find a family when they lose theirs. But they won't necessarily find family in healthy ways—they will be drawn to anything and anyone who promises the connection and identity the child longs for. Gangs. Drugs. Video games. Food. Risky people and relationships. Children grieving the loss of family will look to someone to provide family for them, and they will reach out to the first available person or thing they perceive to be safe.

You and your family must be this child's first available safe thing. You have been assigned by God to meet this child's need for stability. But providing stability, while intuitive on some level, is not such an easy feat. Your child's heart is wounded and perhaps resistant to your attempts to love her. Understanding her wounds might be difficult for you, especially if your experiences with family have been different from your child's.

Longing for Family

An old Welsh word describes the deep longing of children who have lost a family: *Hiraeth* means homesickness for a home to which you cannot return or a yearning for a home that never existed. Take a moment to let *hiraeth* settle into your spirit. *My child yearns for a home to which she cannot return or a home that never existed.*

Hiraeth is what your child feels every day. She has an intense ache in her heart for home. An intense longing for family. She wanders about, driven by her heart's longing, trying to find her place.

When children lose stability, they crave it and seek it for the rest of their lives.

You can't give back to your child her first family. But you can establish a new family to which she belongs. Your family, her new family, will never replace her first family—nor should it. Both she and you know that. But your family can anchor your child's wandering heart by giving her the stability she craves.

Model and teach stable family dynamics.

You intuitively know to provide stability to your child. In fact, you're already doing it—or at least trying your best! Of course, your family is not perfect. It's not about perfection; it's about intention and consistency. Work to create a peaceful environment in your home. Create family traditions—even simple, silly ones. Eat together regularly. (Not that you must eat dinner together every night...let's be realistic! But can you plan onc or two special family meals each week? Consider making them fun family traditions, like pizza Fridays or Saturday morning pancakes.) Play games together, laugh, and have regular family outings.

If you are married, work at making your relationship with your spouse a priority. Two parents who are unified friends walking a life journey together provide the most stable foundation for children.

Don't be afraid to talk about your child's family loss.

Children often postpone their grief until a safe time, when a trusted attachment figure is emotionally available.[4] Now is the time. Don't be afraid to bring up her family loss. Do so gently and respectfully, but do it. Providing the opportunity to talk about loss of family helps your child grieve. It also assures her that you are not jealous of her emotional attachment to her first family or threatened by it. Talking about it is a way to meet her need, not yours. Your child senses your attunement, and she is more likely to talk about her feelings.

Use family language in your home.

Language is powerful because it shapes the way we think about ourselves and the world. Language also helps shape our own personal identities, both through our internal self-talk and what we hear externally from others. A lot of negative, loss-filled self-talk is already running through your child's brain. Counteract that negativity by affirming the truth of God's Word and the truth of who your child is in your family: "We are a family. This is your home. You belong here. You always have a place at this table. You are the child born of my heart. You are part of this family forever."

Consistently assure your child that her first family members love her forever.

The biggest fear your child carries with her *hiraeth* is that her first family members didn't love her. *If Mommy loved me, why did she leave us? If Daddy loved me, why couldn't he give up his drugs?* The truth is that all parents love their children, even if they are terrible parents. Assure your child of this truth: She is forever loved by all her families—birth family, first family, present family, forever family, blended family, adult family, chosen family—regardless of their behavior. Forever loved.

Consistent assurance to your child that she is forever loved by all her families empowers her to accept multiple families in her life. Children don't yet have the years to know that a normal part of life is to be a member of many families. It was never God's plan for a child to live with her birth parents for the rest of her life. God established the "leave and cleave" principle, which means that a child would eventually leave her first family to establish her own: "This is why a man leaves his father and mother and is united to his wife, and they become one flesh" (Genesis 2:24). A child's understanding that she may have many families in her life is not meant to discount her grief at the loss of her first family. Rather, it is to give her an openness to accept the new families to which she also belongs.

When Your Child's Longing for Home Is Hard for You

I imagine you, dear parent, reading this chapter with fresh eyes about the grief your child feels over the loss of her family. You would not be reading this book nor parenting this child if it were not for love—love you have for your child, love for a new spouse, or love for hurting children in general. Because of your love, you are susceptible to feeling your own hurt, especially if parenting this child is difficult. You might have very different feelings about your child's first family than your child does, especially if your interactions with your child's first family have been full of conflict or disappointment. You might even have lost a family, too, when your child lost hers. These experiences can bring up even deeper feelings, including inadequacy, loneliness, or fear that your child won't love you.

You might be trying to push away your feelings because you want to be fully present to meet your child's needs. If you are feeling this way today, please know that your feelings are 100 percent normal and acceptable. It can be so very difficult to facilitate family for a child who has lost a family. But just as parents can love more than one child, children can love more than one family. This is the nature of love—the more love is given, the more it grows. Give it some time and don't give up. And take care of you. You have permission to take care of yourself emotionally, physically, and spiritually. You need this...and your child needs you to be at your best too.

Jada loves her foster mom so much. Foster mom is Mommy. But in her little heart, she will always love her birth parents. She will always love her half siblings. She will want to know them and spend time with them. There are spiritual and physical ties to all families, especially birth families, and these ties can never be severed. You wouldn't want them to be severed, because they make up part of who your child is.

There are spiritual ties to *all* families, including yours. Every day, with your love and care, you are strengthening your parent-child bond, an anchor that can never be uprooted.

Jesus,

I see my child's hiraeth, *her longing for home and family. It breaks my own heart to witness my child's* hiraeth, *because I cannot fix it. But you can fix it, Jesus. You alone can satisfy it, and I ask you to meet my child's heart needs in this very moment. I invite your presence into this home, Jesus. Enter each room, sit and laugh with us at our dining room table, and let your peace be the warm fragrance that fills our home. Give me wisdom to know how to love my child, especially during the difficult moments. In Jesus's name, we are a family established by God, and this child is part of our family forever.*

Amen.

Q: What if my child rejects my attempts to facilitate family?

A: When children lose a family, their hearts are broken by the first people they loved and trusted. It is normal for these children to reject future attempts at love, bonding, and family connection. The risk of rejection and abandonment again is too much, so the child psychologically protects herself by rejecting you first.

The only answer is...hang in there. You must never give up. The only way to salve the pain is to provide consistent love and stability, even if your child seemingly hates you. Your child may never change her feelings or behavior toward you, but you will never know unless you try. God has chosen you to give your child her best opportunity to heal the first-family wound. It will be the most difficult thing you ever do, but I promise, being "Jesus with skin" to a brokenhearted child will be the most worthwhile thing you could ever imagine doing.

Steps Toward Healing

Draw Strength from This Chapter

- Loss of stability is the greatest loss for children who have lost a family.
- Your child needs stable family dynamics; strive to provide them.
- A child's understanding that she may have many families in life gives her an opening to accept the new families to which she also belongs.

What You Can Do Right Now

- Pray the chapter prayer over your child.
- Meditate on Hebrews 6:19. Speak it out loud several times: "We have this hope as an anchor for the soul, firm and secure." Write out the things that you hope for your family (for Jesus to fill your home, for a strong family connection, and so on) in Jesus's name. Speak the verse out loud again, inserting those hopes: "We have Jesus filling our home as an anchor for our souls, firm and secure. In Jesus's name, we have family connection filling our home as an anchor for our souls, firm and secure." This verse has now become a faith-filled, powerful statement about what you hope for your family in Jesus. Speak these statements out loud in your home and over your child.
- Plan some personal self-care time this week, especially if parenting your child has been difficult. Have coffee with a trusted friend, go hiking, or do something to help you rest and connect with others outside your home.

Activities You Can Do This Week with Your Child

- Ask your child to construct a visual for your Hebrews 6:19 hopeful statements. Place the picture in a family area of your home.
- Create a life book for your child (depicting the child's history from birth until present, with room in the book for the future), asking your child to participate in the creation of the book. Even young children can help you; older children and teens may want to take the lead on their life books. Encourage your child to participate in any way she wishes.
- Arrange a meeting or reunion with members of your child's first family if possible and appropriate. Go with your child to the meeting. If it's not appropriate for you to see the family members due to conflict or other issues, then wait patiently while your child visits them. Speak well of the meeting and your child's first family members. Assure your child of her first family's love for her by giving specific examples: "I noticed how your birth father smiled so big when he saw you. You are so precious to him!"
- Find some old family photos or photos of your child with her first family. Find one or two special photos to frame. Give these photos as a gift to your child.

14

When to Get Professional Help

Wisdom Principle

Get professional help if you need it.

The way of fools seems right to them,
but the wise listen to advice.

PROVERBS 12:15

Quinn, a sixth-grade girl, goes to school every day feeling hopeless and alone. One year ago, Quinn and her mother were in a car accident. Her mother died. The long, deep scar across Quinn's left shoulder reminds her every day of her pain and loss. That scar is the outward reminder of the deeper scar in her heart. Her father is devastated, grieving, and now unsure of how to parent his daughter alone—and has become consumed with working on projects in the garage. Quinn eats alone every night. Her grades are slipping, and she doesn't want to go to school. Today Quinn told her only friend that she just doesn't see the point to school, life...or anything.

Like many grieving children, Quinn has reached a very difficult point. Even though it's been a year since her great loss, her heart hasn't healed. In fact, her grief has worsened. Quinn and her father need some help, and fast. You and your child might be experiencing the same thing. This chapter's wisdom principle is also our next parenting skill, which is to get professional help if you need it.

PARENTING SKILL

Get professional help if you need it.

God's Healing Comes in Many Forms

Christian culture is sometimes skeptical of professional mental health resources. I've heard many Christians say that mental health is really spiritual health and that God is the one who solves people's problems: "Turn it over to Jesus. Pray. Confess, repent, and receive forgiveness." These are beautiful aspects of one's faith expression, but the underlying assumption can be that God heals only through outwardly religious practices.

God *is* the solver of problems, and Jesus Christ is the Healer of broken hearts—and he often uses various methods in the healing process. Our wisdom verse for this chapter says that the wise listen to advice (Proverbs 12:15). God can use anyone to bring us wisdom and sound counsel. God has given us science as a tool. As Christians, we are free to use the tools of science, medicine, and professional counseling to support our healing process.

I think the resistance to psychological methods is all about fear. People often fear that they might be labeled "crazy" if they seek professional counseling. There's a big stigma around being diagnosed with a mental disorder. Christians may also fear that their faith and values will be misunderstood or even mocked by a professional counselor. Christians may worry that a non-Christian counselor might undermine their child's faith. And perhaps Christians' deepest fear is that they aren't good Christians if they need professional help. They didn't trust God enough. Or they must have fallen out of God's favor if he hasn't healed them yet.

I am a Christian, and I grew up in a conservative church. I'm also a licensed professional counselor, and I have worked in the mental health field for more than 20 years. I understand why Christians might have these fears, but they simply aren't valid.

The foundation of Christian faith is grace (Ephesians 2:8-9). God offers his favor and healing not because of what you've done or will do but because of his all-consuming love for you. No one can earn God's healing, nor can they ever undo it. Healing is God's gift, given in his way and in his time, for his glory and for a greater good that we cannot yet see. And God uses so many creative methods to heal.

Healing is God's gift, given in his way and in his time, for his glory, and for a greater good.

Professional counselors are trained in cultural competence, which means we must work within the confines of clients' (including children's) personal values and perspectives. These values include religion, faith, and spirituality. You can feel confident that licensed mental health professionals are trained not to impose their personal values onto your child, even if their values greatly differ from yours. The counselor should strive to use language, treatment, and practices that honor your Christian beliefs. The counselor should never pathologize or diagnose you or your child in a bad light because of your faith. If the counselor does this, then it becomes a legal and ethical issue. In this case, you should report the counselor to the state licensing board—and find a new one.

Seeking mental and emotional help can be viewed as a sign of weakness. It shouldn't be. Having weaknesses and vulnerabilities is part of being a human. It's also normal to go through very difficult seasons. Great loss certainly would be characterized as a difficult season! If you need professional help, the wise thing to do is seek it.

When to Seek a Professional Counselor

Please don't misunderstand—I'm not negating prayer, Scripture, or the healing power of Christian community. I have seen God heal people from mental health problems and addiction solely through spiritual means. But pastors are often the first to admit they don't have all the answers, and they commonly refer people to professional counselors because some problems are beyond the scope of pastoral ministry. So the question becomes, "Should I seek help for my child in the church or in a professional counseling office?"

How about both? You can seek spiritual counsel at any time, even if you choose to see a professional counselor. Pastors and professional counselors can and often do work collaboratively. At the very least, let your pastor know about your child's great loss. Ask your church's ministerial staff to observe your child, and ask them whether you need professional help. If your child has questions about death, dying, or how a loving God can allow great loss, then I certainly recommend that you engage a pastor. A professional counselor ethically cannot answer those questions and likely would instruct you to seek spiritual counsel for those answers anyway. Spiritual resources often provide effective tools for healing—friendships, support groups, or pastoral care. Seeking the most support possible is good for your child.

Professional counselors offer additional resources that are not available through pastoral care alone. They provide structured support based in current scientific methods, and they can make a psychological diagnosis that can be helpful if your child needs medication or intensive psychotherapy. You should seek a professional counselor when your child has significant life impairment that does not seem to lessen with other support. However, you should seek a professional counselor immediately in the following circumstances:

- *Suicidal ideation.* Children may express this verbally through art or play or through significant isolation or by engaging in music or media with death themes.
- *Self-harm, such as cutting or hurting oneself.* Self-harm is a significant sign of despair and hopelessness, but it also can be a form of maladaptive coping.
- *Dissociation.* This happens when someone's brain cannot process a trauma; the child appears to "leave" emotionally. For example, his eyes can glass over, and he might be unresponsive or inconsolable. Dissociation usually happens in

short episodes, which are prompted by a trigger (reminder) of the trauma or great loss.

- *Psychosis.* This is a break from reality that includes hallucinations or delusions.
- *Severe depression or anxiety.*
- *Substance abuse or addiction.* Yes, even young children can develop addictions. They might not be using cocaine or methamphetamine, but they certainly can develop addiction to substances that change brain chemistry, such as sugar and caffeine. Children can become addicted to video games and other visual stimulation. If adult substances are around the house, such as alcohol or cigarettes, children might experiment with them or begin using them regularly.

Complicated bereavement is another reason to seek professional counseling. This occurs when the acute symptoms of grief have not resolved within six months of the loss. However, the concept of complicated bereavement is controversial, especially for children. Children are prone to have delayed reactions to loss, especially if they are unaware of the permanency of loss and the changes the loss will bring. Children commonly develop emotional and behavioral symptoms months or even years after the loss if the loss was never processed adequately. Given the lapse between the time of the loss and the time when the child's symptoms are present, parents might miss the connection between the child's symptoms and grief. Grief is then misdiagnosed, and the child is not given proper emotional care.

Where to Start

Going back to our example, Quinn would most definitely benefit from professional counseling. But where to start? What kind of counselor should Quinn see, and how will her father find one? Since Quinn is a child in school, the first place to start is with the school counselor.

School Counselors

School counselors are professional counselors who dedicate their lives to helping students succeed personally, academically, and vocationally. They usually work in public schools, but they also can work in other educational settings. The school counselor will observe your child's functioning at school. If an intervention at school is called for, the school counselor will contact you for your permission to engage your child in things such as a peer group, individual check-in times with the school counselor, or a modified schedule or academic plan. Children who need more academic or behavioral support can be placed on an individual education plan (IEP), structured to support your child's academic success.

School counselors provide immediate crisis intervention, stabilization, and ongoing support at school. They offer empathetic behavioral support if your child is having behavior problems at school. They do not engage in psychotherapy, provide a psychological diagnosis, or manage medication. They are trained to work collaboratively with families and other professional counselors, and they can be amazing resources for your child.

Mental Health Counselors

Mental health counselors typically work in private offices or at a community agency. Sometimes school districts contract with mental health counselors to do therapy at the school during school hours, which can be helpful for scheduling and coordination. A mental health counselor will assess and diagnose your child's problem and will provide a holistic perspective that considers medical, social, and cultural factors. The diagnosis comes from the *Diagnostic and Statistical Manual of Mental Disorders* (*DSM*), which is a manual similar to what medical doctors use to diagnose physical problems. Many people fear being stigmatized for having a *DSM* diagnosis or worry that such a diagnosis will follow a child throughout his life. It's important to know that a *DSM* diagnosis indicates a medical problem. It is a snapshot of your child's current functioning, and it does not indicate that your child is sick or will never recover. It is very common for a *DSM* diagnosis to go into remission or be completely remediated after successful counseling.

Once your child is diagnosed, the counselor will provide psychotherapy. The terms and process of therapy will be written into a treatment plan. Depending on the age of your child, the counselor might involve you in sessions, or the counselor may consult with you after sessions. Mental health counselors who work with children should be skilled in play therapy because children process their emotions through their behavior and play rather than language. However, older children and teens who have more abstract verbal abilities may prefer talk therapy to play therapy.

Psychologists

Psychologists have doctoral degrees, and they specialize in evaluation as well as psychotherapy. A psychological evaluation is helpful in extreme cases, such as when symptoms are life-threatening. A mental health counselor will let you know if a psychological evaluation is needed and can refer you to a psychologist.

Once your child is in therapy, your work doesn't end. In fact, you have a very active role in the therapy's success! First, be positive and hopeful about the experience. Tell your child how proud you are of him for working hard on his grief. Don't ever mock therapy, and don't allow anyone else to mock therapy in front of your child. Sometimes people joke about therapy, and TV and other media are fraught with psychobabble jokes. Humor is important in the healing process, but for now, focus on encouraging your child in his process.

You can support the counselor by ensuring that your child attends all scheduled sessions. Consult with the counselor, especially if you see any behavioral changes (either positive or negative). You have a legal right to ask for your child's therapy records. Inspect them and ask for the records to be changed or updated if there is any incorrect information. If your child has been given a mental health diagnosis, ask the counselor to document the diagnosis at termination. This is important so that you, your child, and any future treatment providers will know the mental status of your child when counseling was completed. And finally, remember who this counseling is for—your child. If you need counseling, it's perfectly okay to get it—in fact, it's a very courageous act to do so! Ask your child's counselor for a referral to a counselor who can support you as the parent of a grieving child.

Wise Parents Listen to Advice

The thought of intense grief issues, such as depression and psychosis, can be really scary for parents. Dear parent, I want to encourage you once again that your child is going to be okay. Professional counselors are well trained, and they can help. They see these types of issues every day, and they know how to work with them.

Grieving children need to process their grief. Ignoring that process can impact your child for a long time. Knowing the right information is the first step in getting your child the kind of help he needs. The Bible says that wise parents listen to advice (Proverbs 12:15). The first source of wisdom is from God. Listen to him first. If he directs you toward professional advice, take action as soon as possible.

Jesus,

My child needs some help. Please give me the wisdom to know if I should find a professional counselor. Help me navigate this process and guide me to the right counselor. Open my child's heart to the counseling process and provide any other resources we need, such as finances and transportation. Help me listen to wise advice and use it to parent my child wisely. I feel afraid for my child, Jesus. Please give me your peace. I know you are here, and I sense your presence.

Amen.

Q: How do I find a professional counselor?

A: Finding a professional counselor can be a challenge, especially if you have never sought one before. The first thing to look for is a counselor who has the proper training and credentials. Your counselor should be licensed as a professional in good standing—a licensed professional counselor (LPC), licensed marriage and family therapist (LMFT), licensed clinical social worker (LCSW), or licensed psychologist. Some states license pastoral counselors, which means the pastoral counselor has a background in therapy as well as religion. But pastoral counselors usually do not provide psychological assessment and diagnosis (which may or may not be beneficial, depending on your circumstances).

Second, look for a counselor who is a good fit for you and your child. Does your child like the counselor and want to go? Do you like the counselor? Can you afford the counseling through the counselor's acceptance of your health insurance or willingness to work out a payment plan? The working relationship between you, your child, and the counselor is very important because the quality of the therapeutic relationship is the best predictor of a good treatment outcome.

Third, look for a counselor who is experienced in working with children and grief. Ask the counselor if she is current on the research about grief and how that knowledge and experience will be woven into the counseling process.

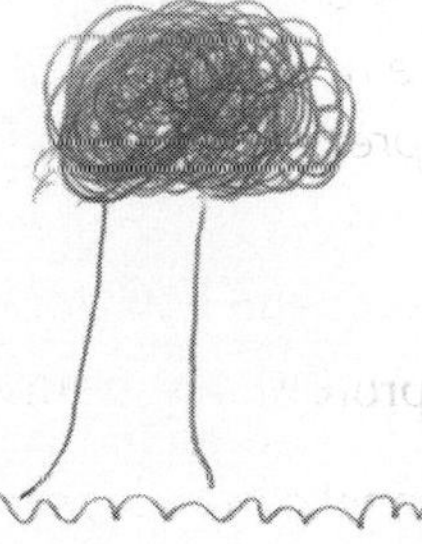

Art by Cynthia, age 9

Steps Toward Healing

Draw Strength from This Chapter

- Remember that God uses many creative methods to heal—both inside and outside the church.
- Seek a professional counselor when your child has significant life impairment that does not seem to lessen with other support.
- Don't hesitate to seek professional counseling if you feel the need for it or godly and wise people are encouraging you toward it.

What You Can Do Right Now

- Pray the chapter prayer over your child.
- Meditate on Proverbs 12:15. Ask God to remind you of wise people who can help you. Write down a list of these people and contact them this week.
- Ask the Lord for guidance as to whether you should seek a professional counselor or spiritual support. Write out the names of some potential professional and spiritual support resources.
- Draw a timeline to track your child's emotional and behavioral symptoms. Start the timeline with your child's birth and include the great loss and any additional stressors, major adjustments, or traumas. Note the years and dates if you know them. Now fill in any emotional or behavioral symptoms you have observed in your child, noting times when they have seemed more apparent. Share this timeline with your child's counselor. This timeline also will be important to see if counseling is helping; your child's symptoms should reduce with effective counseling.

- Check your health insurance benefits for mental health care. Using the guidelines above, do some online research to find counselors in your area who accept your insurance and who you think would be a good fit for your child. If you have decided to pursue professional counseling, call one of them and schedule an initial screening appointment. This appointment does not commit you to working with this counselor; it is just an appointment to see if the counselor would be a good fit.

Activities You Can Do This Week with Your Child

- Visit the school counselor with your child if you determine that your child could benefit from professional support. (You might want to schedule a 20-minute appointment after school to avoid interrupting your child's school day.) The purpose of this visit is to check in to see how your child is functioning at school. Talk about ways the counselor can work with your child to provide support during the school day. Support at school might be all your child needs at this time; the school counselor might be able to help you determine if more counseling is needed and provide you with referrals to a mental health counselor.
- Talk with your child about the possibility of seeing a professional counselor. Explain why you feel that a counselor would be helpful: "I think it would be helpful if you talked with someone special about your really big feelings." If your child does not want to go to counseling, but you feel it would be beneficial, ask your child to go with you to an initial screening appointment. Counselors who work with children are skilled at dealing with children's resistance, and they can help calm your child's anxieties about counseling.

- Try to schedule something special that your child enjoys after each of your child's counseling appointments, such as going out to eat or going to the park. This special time will help your child look forward to counseling days.

15

Let the Little Children Come

Wisdom Principle

Get the spiritual support you need.

Jesus said, "Let the little children come to me, and do not hinder them, for the kingdom of heaven belongs to such as these."

MATTHEW 19:14

I experienced my first great loss at age 16. My father's job required my family to relocate three hours away. A move might not seem like a big deal to most, but it sure was a big deal for me. My family experienced a lot of financial and emotional stress during that season, and my brother and I were in the throes of adolescence. It was just rocky all around. With the move came a new school and a drastically new way of life—all before cell phones and the internet! I was disconnected from my friends and support system. I felt really lonely, hopeless, and afraid.

My life as I knew it was gone, and I couldn't see a way forward.

My saving grace—literally—was a church youth group. For the first time in my life, I had a pastor who was dedicated solely to meeting kids' needs for emotional and spiritual support. Youth group was fun. And it helped me make new friends. I began to develop new dreams and goals for my life, and I eventually found my way—my new normal.

There is a healing strength within a faith community. But as we've discussed throughout this book, grieving children have special needs. I had grown up as a church kid, even attending Christian schools most of the time. But despite the support I received at my youth group, I struggled to understand how a loving God could allow this major challenge for me and my family. The well-worn, churchy answers didn't always make sense. And I didn't feel free to ask the hard questions without being perceived as being disrespectful or rebellious.

Church can be a healing place for kids, but it can also be a tough place. Depending on the religious climate, there can be a lot of pressure. Or confusion. There's sin theology, where kids might feel that they can't or won't measure up. And then there's the issue of hell: *Am I going to hell if I'm bad or I question God?* Church brings with it all these issues for kids, and now we're going to add another big one. Great loss.

Grief adds a whole new layer to church for kids. Your child is not only experiencing the great loss but also might have concerns about death and dying, heaven and hell, angels and visitations, and the like. Children can feel a lot of shame about these issues, but this shame is the opposite of what Jesus told his disciples children need (Matthew 19:14). In this verse, we see Jesus vehemently resisting methods of shaming and withholding children. Instead, Jesus makes it clear that adults are not to do or say anything to hold children back from coming to him and knowing him.

For a grieving child, church can be a sacred place of safety, or it can be a place of confusion and fear. Christian adults mean well, but we don't always know how to speak the language that little broken hearts understand. Other church kids may not understand your child's grief and may make hurtful comments out of ignorance. But Jesus made it clear that he loves children and wants them to come to him. Parents of grieving children (and all Christians!) need a few extra strategies for helping children come to Jesus.

Our grieving children's spiritual development depends on it.

For a grieving child, church can be a sacred place of safety, or it can be a place of confusion and fear.

Common Faith Experiences After Loss

Grieving people—including children—often have unique faith experiences. The great loss triggers thoughts and feelings about life and death that weren't there before. To resolve these thoughts and feelings, the griever must make personal meaning from the loss. The two most common faith experiences are renewal of faith and cessation of faith.

Renewed Faith

A renewal of faith happens when the great loss triggers new thinking about life and death: *Where did my loved one go? Where will I go after I die? What is the purpose for my life? What should I do in the time I have left on this earth?* People who have a renewal of faith can accept that God makes the big decisions about life and death even if they don't like the decisions. A renewal of faith also can result from a fear of the afterlife, such as being afraid of going to hell, or a sobering evaluation of one's current lifestyle. Memorial services often are held in churches, and they can prompt new thoughts about the spiritual realm. While generally a positive experience, a renewal of faith can create some difficulty if the faith practice becomes so all-consuming that other life priorities are ignored or if it's prompted by fear.

Adults might miss the fact that when children experience a great loss, they may desire to renew their faith or find new faith. Kids often do what they're told, so they follow the family religious norms. But great loss is different. It shakes the very foundation of a child's security, and faith can help your child make meaning from her loss. Faith can be a great source of comfort during the mourning season. It also can be a way to provide life direction and wisdom, which is important if your child lost a source of wisdom (such as a parent or grandparent). Your child may sense these things intuitively even if she does not know how to outwardly express them.

After loss, children may desire to renew their faith or find new faith.

Children usually express curiosity in something by asking questions. It's the same with their interest in faith. They may comment about something they've observed, or they may tell you a story about something that happened to them—or a friend—at church. Take note of what your child talks about, especially if there is a theme around God or spiritual things. Support your child's faith interest in whatever way you can, especially by talking with her and listening to her. Be willing to go to church with your child, even if that is not your custom. (What's a couple of hours on the weekend? It's a nice time to connect with your child. Make it a family day and go out for lunch afterward. Or go fishing...or both!)

The Interruption or End of Faith

The second spiritual experience, a cessation of faith, happens when the griever is not able to reconcile belief in God with the great loss: *If there is a God, and he loves me, why did he let this great loss happen?* Sometimes it's hard to believe in a loving God when experiencing a tragedy. There is an underlying assumption that life should be fair and that God's job is to ensure that fairness. But life clearly wasn't fair, and a child can conclude that God cannot be trusted. The result is a loss of faith and even a refusal to believe that God exists.

Children experiencing a cessation of faith may feel angry. They may feel alone, and they may feel like the very stability of their lives has been ripped out from underneath them. If their family or their other social supports stop believing in God, they may pick up on the emotional climate and decide they don't believe in God either. They may express their feelings outwardly (if they feel safe to do so), or they may hold their feelings inside and not say anything at all. In this case, you and your child might have a power struggle about church attendance and spiritual matters. You also might see an intentional movement away from spiritual things, such as seeking non-Christian friends or activities.

Spiritual experiences are unique to each individual, and they can vary in intensity. People in the same family can have different spiritual experiences. Perhaps you are experiencing a cessation of faith from the great loss, whereas your child is experiencing a renewal of faith. Or maybe it's the other way around; more than ever, you are dedicated to your faith, whereas your child flat-out refuses to have anything to do with God. If you and your child are in different places spiritually, remember this is normal. Spiritual beliefs are very deep and personal, even for children. Work even harder at attunement, realizing your child's faith expression is part of her way of making sense of the great loss.

Christian parents of grieving children sometimes fear their children won't recover from the great loss and will eventually reject God. Or they fear their children will pretend to walk with God on the outside but fail to have a relationship with God in their hearts. The best way to handle a child's cessation of faith is to model the way you want her to go (Proverbs 22:6). Modeling has to do with leadership by example, not punishment or power struggles. Envision how you would like your child's faith to be and then practice those behaviors in a way that your child can see. You don't need to punish her for having conflicted spiritual thoughts and feelings. Instead, listen to your child and affirm her for who she is, even if you disagree. (Requiring your child to attend church activities is okay if this is a family expectation, but don't punish her for not liking it.)

If you and your child are in different places spiritually, remember this is normal. Spiritual beliefs are very deep and personal, even for children.

Don't force your child to participate in religious experiences that scare her, such as the laying on of hands, speaking in tongues, baptism, communion, or the like. Religious rituals are sacred and beautiful, and they can be deeply healing. But if your child is angry, fearful, or resistant, the experience will be harmful. That's exactly the opposite of what you—and God—intended, and it's the quickest way to get your kid to slam the church doors behind her the minute she's old enough to drive a car. When children are encouraged to feel what they feel, think what they think, and say what they want to say, they will tell you when they want to participate in religion. Remember that spiritual beliefs are deeply personal, and respect your child's choice of how to develop her relationship with God...even though she's still a child.

And then. Radically trust God with your child's heart. Remember, Jesus is the Healer, and you are not. If God already knows all the days of your child's life (Psalm 139:16), he can handle a little spiritual crisis. He's got this.

God always makes the first move. He moves toward us through the Holy Spirit, and the Holy Spirit is the one who changes our hearts (Ezekiel 36:26). We cannot receive God without his Spirit moving in us and through us. As parents, our first faith responsibility for our children is to pray for them. So pray for your child. Pray in faith that the Holy Spirit will move toward your child's heart and transform it. Pray that your child will find her own special relationship with God. God wants a relationship with your child even more than you want your child to attend church or make a spiritual commitment. *He is not going to let go of your child.*

> God wants a relationship with your child...He is not going to let go of your child.

Church, You, and Your Child

I'm a pastor's wife, which means that church ministry is a daily activity in our household. I have a deep respect for those who minister to children and youth. It's hard and often thankless work, and they do it out of an absolute love for kids. They also sense a strong calling from God toward their work. Parent, remember that your child is deeply loved and valued, both by Jesus and the church ministers who interact with her. Most children's ministers want to know how they can best love your child, especially during a difficult season, such as a time of grief. We've arrived at our next parenting skill, which is to elicit spiritual support.

PARENTING SKILL

Elicit spiritual support.

Figuring out how to navigate church life for your grieving child is challenging. What should you do if another child in Sunday school says or does something that hurts your child? What if simply walking into church overwhelms your child with reminders of the funeral? You are not alone; children's ministers are here to help. Here are a few simple strategies for working with them.

Tell your child's helpers that she has special needs right now.

Communicating with your child's ministers will let them know what is going on with your child and your family. They can give your child extra care and pray for her. They can use wisdom as they develop lessons and activities, and they can have a plan in place if your child needs a time-out or needs to see you.

You don't have to explain the great loss.

It is enough to inform church ministers that your child has experienced a great loss and is in a season of mourning or adjustment. Whether to share more details is for you and your child to decide. Share information on a need-to-know basis. If you believe that sharing the details of the great loss will help your child have a positive church experience, then share them. If not, keep them private and allow your child to share those details in her own way and in her own time.

Regularly check with your child about church and God.

Going to church can be comforting for your child, or it can be distressing—perhaps even both! Ask your child about her experience during church activities. Let her know she can share anything with you without being afraid. She might have questions, or she might not have anything to say. Try not to make assumptions, and let your child process her feelings in the way she needs to. Ask the Holy Spirit to anoint and direct your conversations and to give you the wisdom you need to respond.

At all times, know that you can advocate for your child. If your child is not getting what she needs at church, speak up and ask for what she needs. This advocacy will not take your child's pain or choices away, but it will show her that you are walking this journey beside her. Your child needs to be seen, heard, and comforted, especially by her spiritual supporters. This is what Jesus meant when he said, "Let the little children come."

Come and Be Loved

God established the church so we could get to know him better. It's also a place we can experience community and relationship. Hebrews 10:24-25 says we are to "spur one another on toward love and good deeds, not giving up meeting together, as some are in the habit of doing, but encouraging one another—and all the more as you see the Day approaching." Let your church love you and your child during this season of grief. Your community stands in the gap when you can't, especially when you need extra support.

If your church isn't supportive or isn't enriching your relationship with Jesus, find a different church. If you haven't been to church in a while and you're worried about being perceived as an unfaithful Christian...don't be. Welcoming someone back to church after a long hiatus is exciting. There is no shame, no guilt—only celebration and relationship. Ministers feel honored to walk beside a child or family that needs a little extra love and support. It's our calling as well as our privilege. So come.

Jesus,

I so desperately want my child to love you and follow you. Right now, I am struggling to know how to provide the best spiritual example during this journey. It's hard to trust in your plan because you allowed this great loss. But I choose to faithfully help my child come to you. Please move toward us right where we are on this journey. Show us your compassion and understanding. Please give me wisdom to know how to give and receive spiritual support for my child.

Amen.

Q: How do I answer tough spiritual questions about death and loss?

A: Christians have unique beliefs about death and life after death. These beliefs come from the Bible. "Answers to Tough Theological Questions About Death and Loss" on page 199 lists common spiritual questions grieving children may have and answers these questions in child-friendly language.

Steps Toward Healing

Draw Strength from This Chapter

- For grieving children, church can be a sacred place of safety, or it can be a place of confusion and fear.
- Great loss often triggers unique spiritual experiences—renewal of faith or cessation of faith.
- The church can offer love and support to your child during this time of grief if you let it.

What You Can Do Right Now

- Pray the chapter prayer over your child.
- Meditate on Matthew 19:14. What are some ways you can help your child come to Jesus? Jot down a few notes.
- Commit to pray each day that the Holy Spirit will move toward your child, giving her a new heart that is open to God (Ezekiel 36:26).
- Think about the two types of faith experiences after crisis or loss. Have you ever experienced a renewal of faith or a cessation of faith? What was it like? What did you wish someone would have told you during that time? Write out your answers in child-friendly language. Be ready to share your experience with your child if God opens a door for that conversation.

Activities You Can Do This Week with Your Child

- Attend church or a ministry activity together. Afterward, go out for lunch or ice cream and talk about the experience. Ask your child what she liked about church and what she didn't like. Let her know that whatever she feels is okay.

But also affirm that Jesus loves her and wants a relationship with her.

- Ask your child to pray with you, and pray this prayer together regularly: "Dear Jesus, we are thankful that you love us. Help me understand why [the great loss] happened. Thank you for your comfort, especially when I feel sad or mad or scared. Amen."

Jesus loves me,
this I know

Art by Zane, age 7

16

Great Will Be Your Children's Peace

Wisdom Principle

Jesus will bring your child peace.

All your children will be taught by the Lord,
and great will be their peace.

Isaiah 54:13

It's not fair. How could this happen? Why my child? Why us?

These questions come from a place of pain. A place of great loss. A place of confusion because your whole way of looking at the world—what you believe about people and maybe even what you believe about God—has been shaken to its very core. Others might try to answer these questions for you by giving you the stock Christian answers: "Just pray. The Lord knows. Your loved one is better off. Your child will be okay. Time heals all wounds." Yes, these people genuinely care, but their answers reveal that they don't know the depth of pain that great loss brings. They just don't get it.

Every day in my work and ministry, I sit with people in pain. I've experienced great loss myself. I can tell you honestly that there are no answers. Or at least no good answers. Because frankly, there is no good reason for great loss. What happened to your child and your family is an egregious tragedy. I don't know why it happened to your child, and I don't know the reasons you are now assigned to parent a grieving child.

But I do know this. God sees and hears everything, especially things that are not fair. He absolutely hates injustice. God cherishes children, and he specifically helps children who have lost parents and families. They are the apple of his eye. God holds accountable those who hurt children. And God hates injustice, death, and grief so much that he promises to make it right.

Is this difficult for you to believe? Consider the story of Isaiah. He was a prophet who lived in ancient Judah, a country that struggled to stay faithful to God. Judah experienced a lot of pain because the people refused to walk in God's ways. Eventually Judah's bad choices left them vulnerable to the aggressive superpower at the time—Assyria. Many people of Judah lost their homes, their children, their freedom...and probably their sanity.

God cherishes children, and he specifically helps children who have lost parents and families.

As city after city fell, the defeated inhabitants of Judah suffered with despairing and broken hearts. Isaiah watched as his nation started crumbling, and his journey through grief was undoubtedly a hard one, just like yours. His heart was surely broken. But Isaiah had a special assignment. As a prophet, he heard and saw things directly from God. God told Isaiah he was watching from on high. God saw all the tears of his people, and he grieved with them. God told Isaiah he was going to rescue, comfort, and heal Judah even though she had turned her back on him.

Isaiah wrote down everything God told him to say. And he preached God's words of redemption to the people.

Some people received the good news, but others probably thought Isaiah was crazy. How would life ever be good again? Jerusalem was the only city left. The people were surely beginning to feel hopeless. They were tired. And they were angry. The very God they were supposed to trust, the God who was supposedly in control, had allowed their nation to suffer great loss.

Imagine Isaiah waking up every morning, his heart heavier than his limbs. He could see the first light of the sunrise, yet he numbly wondered at the paradox of a new day when the future felt so completely dark and stuck. His family was hurting. His neighbors had little hope. Isaiah himself may have carried anger and frustration at a God whom he was supposed to be able to trust. And yet he clearly heard the voice of the Lord. A voice so big, so powerful, that he had no other choice but to swing his legs over the side of his bed, sit up, and prepare mentally and emotionally once again to do the task the Lord had assigned him.

Care for the grieving.

Can you relate? Isaiah was like you. His future often looked bleak, and the outcome was potentially devastating, especially to the most innocent—the children. Children who never did anything to deserve such great loss.

But here's the redemptive part. Every one of Isaiah's numb, cold, empty mornings were short sentences of a much, much bigger story.

> Surely he took up our pain
> and bore our suffering,
> yet we considered him punished by God,
> stricken by him, and afflicted.
> But he was pierced for our transgressions,
> he was crushed for our iniquities;
> the punishment that brought us peace was on him,
> and by his wounds we are healed (Isaiah 53:4-5).

"By his wounds we *are* healed"—present tense, not past tense. Isaiah was referring to a future Messiah healing his people's pain in the present. This story wasn't just about Judah's redemption. The bigger story was about Jesus Christ, who was coming because the world was broken. Hurting. Grieving. Mourning. Jesus was going to heal all of it. Here and now. For everyone.

The Greatest Story in the World Still Needs a Messenger

> How beautiful on the mountains
> are the feet of those who bring good news,

who proclaim peace,
    who bring good tidings,
    who proclaim salvation,
who say to Zion,
    "Your God reigns!" (Isaiah 52:7).

Isaiah didn't understand all the details of the bigger story. Amid his looming tragedy, he couldn't have seen how those small sentences would ever make sense to himself or anyone else. He just got up and walked the journey God asked him to walk. He wrote down God's words and shared the message with the people. Even though it was exhausting. Even though he was lonely. Even though it seemed like this painful tragedy would never end.

God saw and heard it all. He cherished his children, and he watched over them. And he came through. God knew the great loss wasn't fair, and he hated every minute of Judah's tragedy. And in his time and in his way, God redeemed Judah. He delivered Jerusalem from the mighty Assyrian army. He made it right.

Isaiah was in an uncomfortable position, yet his message from God was unmistakable: Whisper peace in the face of fear. Speak good news and stability over the looming devastation. Announce impending redemption to the shackles of captivity. Proclaim that the Lord God Almighty is Judah's benevolent and rightful king. Even though God seems nowhere to be found, proclaim in faith that *our God reigns*.

Isaiah knew God was sovereign. So he kept sharing God's words. Day after difficult day, even though he could not see the end of the day. He continued not because he wanted to but because he trusted God. When we have experienced great loss, sometimes our faith in something bigger is the only thing we have left. So Isaiah put his tired feet to the cold ground, and he faithfully walked his difficult journey.

Isaiah was the messenger.

And...how beautiful. How beautiful a story to tell. A much, much bigger story than what Isaiah could ever conceive. The story of redemption and healing *for the entire world.*

When we have experienced great loss, sometimes our faith in something bigger is the only thing we have left.

God was the author, not Isaiah. And God's story didn't end with the coming of the Messiah. No. God's story *spread to the entire world* through Jesus. Look at the very next chapter, Isaiah 54, where God said what it's going to be like when the Messiah reappears to stay. Safety. Stability. Healing. Prosperity. And the peace that Jesus, the Prince of Peace, establishes for everybody. Forever.

The most epic of all epic stories.

So why your child's great loss? There isn't an answer to that question. But the redemption? The redemption is your child's story. His epic story, written by Jesus Christ, the master author. The story of his healing. The story of his salvation. The story of his peace.

PARENTING SKILL

Be the messenger of Jesus Christ's love and healing.

It's been quite a journey for you. I imagine that reading this book has been as much an emotional experience as it has been a learning one. It's not easy working through grief, especially your own child's grief. As you recognized the feelings and experiences unique to your grieving child, you've realized the depth of pain your child's loss has brought him. I know that you have carried that burden of pain too.

As you care for a grieving child whom you love desperately, you can feel lonely. God knits our children in our hearts so tightly that their pain will always tear at our own hearts too. You are not alone. Jesus the Healer has been right here on every page. Every step, seeing you. Loving you. Giving you wisdom about what to do and what to say. Teaching you new skills to guide your grieving child. And whispering hope and encouragement, even on the most difficult days.

Your wisdom and skills make you the perfect one to take a leading role in your child's epic story. Like Isaiah, *you* are the messenger of Isaiah 52:7. You are the messenger of good news, peace, and salvation through Jesus. You're not responsible for fixing your child. You were never supposed to be your child's healer, and you never could be. Because Jesus is the Healer. He's got that role. That's his part in your child's story. That's what he came to do—to bind up the brokenhearted.

And that's exactly what he's doing, through you. You are the messenger.

God chose you to be your child's parent. Your child didn't ask for this great loss, and neither did you. You may not have even planned to parent this child. You may never have wanted to be a parent. But for heavenly reasons perhaps unknown, God gave you this incredible part in your child's story.

Your role, then, is to be the messenger of God's love, care, and provision. To be the voice of Jesus for him. To acknowledge God's sovereignty even when that acknowledgment feels so completely counterintuitive. To model how God watches over all his children. To give your child hope. And most of all, to introduce him to Jesus, the Healer.

Your child's healing might take time. His story may not be written the way you would have written it. He might have times of struggle, and he might have seasons when his grief is fresh and piercing once again. It's all okay. The timing and method of your child's healing is not your call. It is God's call because he's God. It's hard to understand how God works sometimes. But you can trust him to keep his promises, because he's already proven himself to be a promise keeper.

"Our God reigns" will be the theme of the beautifully written chapters of your child's epic story. Isaiah didn't know how Judah's story would end. But you already know the end of your child's story. Jesus has already written the last page. Your child will become "[an oak] of righteousness, a planting of the Lord for the display of his splendor" (Isaiah 61:3).

Be the messenger for your child. Help him know Jesus, the mender of broken hearts. Because through Jesus, your child will have peace.

And so will you.

All your children will be taught by the LORD,
and great will be their peace (Isaiah 54:13).

Jesus,

It's been a long journey. You have been with us every step of the way. We have arrived at a place of goodness and blessing, and I praise you. Our external circumstances haven't changed, but you have given us peace in our hearts. My child's great loss will always be a part of his life, but it will not overshadow his life, for you have redeemed and healed it. My child will be strong and will fulfill the good purpose you designed for him. I ask for your continued presence in my child's life and mine. Thank you for your comfort, Jesus. Thank you for your healing. Thank you for your peace. And now lead us on to our next step.

Amen.

Q: What if I don't have a relationship with Jesus yet?

A: If you don't know Jesus as your personal Savior yet, would you like to? Becoming a Christian doesn't mean your life will be perfect. You will still have pain and trials. You may even have great loss. But you will have a friend and a Healer to walk with you through them. You also will have the hope and confidence of eternal life. Take a moment to pray and receive his abundant life and healing love:

> Jesus, I believe you are God and the Savior of the world. I want you to be the Lord of my life. Please forgive my sin and teach me to live in a loving, righteous way. Please be my friend and help me with my trials. Give me wisdom. I receive your love and your gift of salvation. Thank you, Jesus.

If you just prayed that prayer for the first time, congratulations! The Bible says that the angels rejoice when people come to

God (Luke 15:7), so that means there's a huge, joyous, heavenly concert going on right now. Make sure you tell another Christian about your decision to accept Jesus as your Savior. Find a local, Christ-following church for support and community as you learn about your new faith.

Steps Toward Healing

Draw Strength from This Chapter

- God sees and cares about your child's grief. He will redeem the great loss.
- You are the messenger of God's love and healing for your child.
- Jesus Christ is the Healer. Knowing Jesus will bring you and your child peace.

What You Can Do Right Now

- Pray the chapter prayer over your child.
- Meditate on Isaiah 54:13. Reflect on this entire journey toward healing. How has God established peace in your home? How has God established peace in your heart and your child's? Jot down a few notes.
- Reflect on what you've learned by reading this book. What have been some of the most healing things for you and your child? What have been some of the most effective strategies for parenting your grieving child? Write them down.
- Meditate on God's promises for grieving children (see below). Thank God for his faithfulness to you and your child through this healing journey.

Activities You Can Do This Week with Your Child

- Get some art paper, nature supplies, and craft supplies. Have your child create or draw a visual of an oak tree planted by a stream of water. Read Isaiah 61:1-3 when your child is finished. Talk about what it means to be "oaks of righteousness, a planting of the LORD for the display of his splendor." Talk about what this visual will mean in your child's life. Use hopeful language.

- Read the following promises and verses out loud to your child. You may need to explain what these promises and verses mean in child-friendly language.

God's Promises for Grieving Children

God cherishes children.

He called a little child to him, and placed the child among them. And he said: "Truly I tell you, unless you change and become like little children, you will never enter the kingdom of heaven. Therefore, whoever takes the lowly position of this child is the greatest in the kingdom of heaven. And whoever welcomes one such child in my name welcomes me" (Matthew 18:2-5).

Children are the apple of God's eye.

In a desert land he found him,
in a barren and howling waste.
He shielded him and cared for him;
he guarded him as the apple of his eye
(Deuteronomy 32:10).[1]

God helps children who have lost parents and families.

But you, God, see the trouble of the afflicted;
you consider their grief and take it in hand.
The victims commit thenselves to you;
you are the helper of the fatherless (Psalm 10:14).

God holds accountable those who hurt children.

> This is what the Lord says:
> "Yes, captives will be taken from warriors,
> and plunder retrieved from the fierce;
> I will contend with those who contend with you,
> and your children I will save" (Isaiah 49:25).

God hates injustice and death.

> The Lord said, "What have you done? Listen! Your brother's blood cries out to me from the ground. Now you are under a curse and driven from the ground, which opened its mouth to receive your brother's blood from your hand. When you work the ground, it will no longer yield its crops for you. You will be a restless wanderer on the earth" (Genesis 4:10-12).

God promises to make it right.

> Adam made love to his wife again, and she gave birth to a son and named him Seth, saying, "God has granted me another child in place of Abel, since Cain killed him" (Genesis 4:25).

Art by Emmalee, age 10

The Next Step

He will command his angels concerning you
to guard you in all your ways.

PSALM 91:11

Another sleepless night. Through teary eyes you look toward the moon spilling its rays all over a dark landscape, and you wonder how the world can just keep on going despite your broken heart. Aching for your child, a child who is hurting. Your heart yearns for anything to soothe your child's pain, but your head knows there is nothing you can do to make it right again.

It's a feeling deeper than loneliness. It's utter helplessness.

Friend, I know your journey has been a lonely one. I know that helpless feeling, and I know the heaviness of your burden. I've walked the same journey for a grieving child that you are walking now. This book grew out of my hope to come alongside you for a small part of your journey. Not to bear your burden but to encourage you as you carry it.

But now our time is short, and our ways must part. You have your road, and I have mine. I leave you with one last bit of encouragement to keep you moving to your promised land. It is a simple but profound piece of wisdom that God knitted in my heart during my healing journey:

Rest.

Parenting—especially parenting a child with extra emotional needs—has no guarantees. It is an assignment to navigate with an unknown destination. It is one of the most supreme acts of faith ever ascribed to humankind. A journey of radical trust in something bigger: something bigger than you, something bigger than your child, and something bigger than any skills or support anyone could ever give you.

It is not with glib Christianese that I tell you about radical trust. Because I hated every step of my journey. Oh, how I fought it. I was pretty upset with God (and everything and everyone else) for a long time. Only in recent years has God brought me to a point in my journey where I have found peace. My peace came when I realized that even though I didn't know where I was going, *I knew that I had arrived at the end of myself.* I wasn't big enough to fix great loss. Even though I was professionally trained as a counselor, had all the skills, knew all the language, prayed fervently, and acted like a Christian...I could not heal, save, or fix my children.

Only Jesus could. And he did, and he is still in the process of healing them. He was faithful to heal—in his way and in his time.

Radical trust meant I had to learn a very, very hard lesson. These children are not my children. They are God's children. He only entrusted them to me so I could steward them while on this earth. And he loves them more than I possibly could. Someone bigger was the boss. He got to call the shots. I could either radically trust him, surrender to him, and experience his peace that passes all understanding, or I could fight the great loss and continue to walk my journey in anger, exhaustion, helplessness, and loneliness.

Either way, he would have healed them. *But I had to choose which path I would walk.*

I finally have chosen radical trust and surrender. My God reigns.

Peace.

Mama, I understand how your heart breaks for your child. Daddy, I understand how helpless you feel. And how long has it been since you have slept sweetly? How long has it been since you awoke refreshed, alert, full of hope and promise for a new day? How long has it been since you let God attend to you in the same way you attend to your precious child?

During my long, sleepless nights, God taught me how to rest. Rest isn't just sleep; it is an intentional connection of our spirit to his Spirit wherein he refreshes us. Through this connection, he gives us life and hope in return for our death and despair.

The quickest way to connection with God's Spirit is through worship. Worship opens the spiritual realms and simultaneously opens our hearts. The Spirit of God descends and fills every fiber of our being. And through that connection, we are fully alive, fully connected, and fully whole. Something shifts, something changes, and it's bigger than us and our pain. We return home, to where our spirits came from.

How long has it been since you let God attend to you in the same way you attend to your precious child?

How do you worship? Open your mouth and sing praise to God. Sing out loud what he brings into your heart. Sing out in faith God's promises of healing for you and your child. Open your Bible and sing Scripture out loud. Insert your name and your child's name into the text as if you were singing a blessing over your child. It doesn't matter how it sounds. To God, worship is the most exquisite poetry. It invokes his favor, his blessing, his love, his protection, his provision, and all his good gifts. (Personally, I love to sing Psalm 91 over my children and family; it is a powerful psalm of protection and provision.)

And so I leave you with this final step. *It's time to rest.* Set down your burden. Take your shoes off and breathe deeply. Worship. Snuggle into God's comfort and surrender all to the keeper of the angels.

A Blessing

Though your days be long and weary,
may each step bring you toward restoration of joy and life.

When you feel alone and thirsty,
may his presence refresh your spirit and renew your strength.

Though your path be steep or meandering,
may you always walk toward the Son on the horizon.

Shalom, peace, my friend, until we meet again.

16 Special Skills for Parenting Grieving Children

Parenting Skill	Wisdom Verse
Learn about grief through your Christian faith and psychological principles.	If any of you lacks wisdom, you should ask God, who gives generously to all without finding fault, and it will be given to you (James 1:5).
Take care of your child, and do not allow your child to be your caretaker.	[Parents], do not embitter your children, or they will become discouraged (Colossians 3:21).
Take extra good care of your child's physical body.	I praise you because I am fearfully and wonderfully made; your works are wonderful, I know that full well (Psalm 139:14).
Communicate about the great loss honestly and with hope.	Speaking the truth in love, we will grow to become in every respect the mature body of him who is the head, that is, Christ (Ephesians 4:15).
Respond to your child's really big feelings.	The Lord does not look at the things people look at. People look at the outward appearance, but the Lord looks at the heart (1 Samuel 16:7).
Attend to your child's heart before providing correction.	No discipline seems pleasant at the time, but painful. Later on, however, it produces a harvest of righteousness and peace for those who have been trained by it (Hebrews 12:11).
Listen but don't stop parenting.	"I know the plans I have for you," declares the Lord, "plans to prosper you and not to harm you, plans to give you hope and a future" (Jeremiah 29:11).
Lovingly educate and support your child as he says goodbye.	Guide me in your truth and teach me, for you are God my Savior, and my hope is in you all day long (Psalm 25:5).
Facilitate a mourning season.	The Lord is close to the brokenhearted, and saves those who are crushed in spirit (Psalm 34:18).

Parenting Skill	Wisdom Verse
Move forward while still remembering the loss.	The memory of the righteous is a blessing (Proverbs 10:7 ESV).
Help children who have lost a parent facilitate an ongoing bond with that parent.	A father to the fatherless, a defender of widows, is God in his holy dwelling (Psalm 68:5).
Help children who have lost a sibling feel connected and purposeful.	God sets the lonely in families, he leads out the prisoners with singing (Psalm 68:6).
Provide stability to children who have lost a family.	We have this hope as an anchor for the soul, firm and secure (Hebrews 6:19).
Get professional help if you need it.	The way of fools seems right to them, but the wise listen to advice (Proverbs 12:15).
Elicit spiritual support.	Jesus said, "Let the little children come to me, and do not hinder them, for the kingdom of heaven belongs to such as these" (Matthew 19:14).
Be the messenger of Jesus Christ's love and healing.	All your children will be taught by the LORD, and great will be their peace (Isaiah 54:13).

Answers to Tough Theological Questions About Death and Loss

Grieving children often have special questions about death and great loss. They might be afraid to ask these questions, or they might ask them at strange times. As a Christian parent, you might feel stuck on how to answer the tough questions. I've listed some questions your child might ask (or wonder about) and suggested answers in child-friendly language. You might have a couple of these questions too! I encourage you to look up the Scripture verses for your own prayer and meditation.

Special thanks to pastors Leif Ford and Ev Denniston for their guidance.

Did my deceased loved one go to hell?

Children may hear about heaven and hell and fear that a deceased loved one went to hell. A child who is afraid of hell should know that God is a God of love. God created everybody to know him, and he doesn't want anyone to go to hell (Ezekiel 18:32; 2 Peter 3:9). It is important to teach children that hell does exist (Psalm 9:17; Matthew 10:28). Hell is a real place for people who reject God. But it is impossible for humans to know the heart of another human (1 Samuel 16:7), and therefore no one can say for sure that a deceased person went to hell.

Ask your child where he heard about heaven and hell and why it sounds scary to him. He may have heard something from another child or from an adult who said something out of ignorance or insensitivity.

You can say to your child, "I'm confident God would have done everything possible to reach out to [name of deceased] so that he knew God. We know that God is good, merciful, and kind. He loves [name of deceased] and doesn't want him to be in hell. We leave those important decisions to God."

If your child heard something inappropriate from someone else, approach that person kindly and gently, explaining the values you are teaching your child about your faith, heaven, and hell. Ask that individual to respect your values and not to make theological comments that your child is not ready to process.

What is heaven, and who goes there?

Children may wonder what heaven is, where it is, and what it takes to get there. Say to your child, "Heaven is a special place where God lives. People who believe that Jesus Christ is the Son of God go to heaven (Acts 16:31). In heaven, we live with God and experience joy all the time."

Why do people die?

People die because our bodies are mortal. "Mortal" means the life on this earth ends sometime. After we die, our bodies become immortal, and people who know God live in heaven with him forever. Say to your child, "Our spirits live forever, but our bodies eventually stop working and die. Even mine, and even yours. The death of our bodies is a normal part of life. I know death might sound scary, but there is nothing to be afraid of. Jesus is always with us. He will help us when it's our time to die. We can look forward to living with God in heaven after we die."

Will I ever see my deceased loved one again?

Say to your child, "In heaven, there will be a reunion of people who know and love God (Isaiah 25:6-8). God will prepare a huge feast, and everyone will celebrate. He will destroy death forever, and he will wipe away everyone's tears. There will be no more pain in heaven, and we will live with [name of deceased] forever, praising God all the time."

Can the deceased see me right now?

There is not a lot of biblical evidence that the deceased can see people on earth or that they visit us. There is some evidence that spirits can be raised through divination (1 Samuel 28:3-25), but God is clear that divination is an unholy and off-limits practice (Leviticus 19:26; Deuteronomy 18:10). However, many grieving people, including children, report having vivid dreams or visitations from the deceased, and your child may have these experiences as well. In times of uncertainty, the Bible says to test the spirits to see if they are from God (1 John 4:1). If the end result is peace and comfort, that experience is likely from God. If the experience leaves chaos, confusion, and fear, that's a sign that the experience is from the enemy (1 Peter 5:6-9).

If your child reports a supernatural encounter with the deceased, ask him if the encounter made him feel better or feel worse. If he felt better, say, "We can trust that peace is from Jesus." If your child reports that he felt worse (especially if he felt confusion, depression, or anxiety), comfort your child, and explain that the bad feelings are not to be trusted. Then pray over your child: "In the name of Jesus, I rebuke any evil spirit that will cause confusion, depression, or fear. I speak peace over [child's name] in the name of Jesus." Continue to pray for your child daily, especially if you suspect the need for spiritual warfare (Ephesians 6:10-20). If intense prayer scares your child, then pray alone (see chapter 15).

Is the great loss my fault?

Sometimes children feel responsible for things that are not their responsibility. It's natural for children to personalize a loved one's death, a loss, or a traumatic event. *Maybe I was bad, or maybe I didn't pray enough.* Death and great loss happen because other people make choices and because our bodies are mortal. Children need to be reminded that they are not responsible, even if they don't wonder about their responsibility out loud. Say to your child, "Some kids might feel like it's their fault that [great loss] happened. I want to make sure that you know it's not your fault. There is nothing you could have done to stop [great loss], and you didn't cause it either. Bad things happen because of other people's choices and because our bodies eventually get sick or die. The good news is that Jesus knows about our sadness and pain, and he heals us."

Why does the great loss feel so bad?

Great loss makes our hearts hurt so much because we loved the person or thing we lost. And they loved us too. Say to your child, "It hurts because you love [name of person] and he will no longer be here with us on earth. God created us with happy feelings and sad feelings. In time, and through God's comfort, the sad feelings will not hurt so much. And it's okay to have happy feelings and do fun things even though you are sad about [great loss]."

And a few questions that parents might be wrestling with too...

If God is such a loving God, why did this great loss happen to my child?

God does not cause bad things to happen. Bad things happen because humans have free will. Free will is the ability to make autonomous choices. Everybody has a free will, including your child.

Think about how you love your child. You would never want to keep your child locked up in his room, limiting all his choices and controlling everything he did. If you did, you would know that if he showed "love" for you, it would not really be love at all. It would be fear. You want your child to love you freely because true love comes from autonomous choice and not control.

The same is true with God. He gave all humans free will because he wants us to choose to love him rather than to be forced to love him. But the dark side of our free will means that people are free to make bad choices along with the good. These bad choices often create deep grief, loss, and trauma for other people (Romans 5:12).

No human caused the loss my child is experiencing, so it had nothing to do with free will. Why did God still allow the loss, knowing my child would experience so much pain?

God made the world to be perfect. This was his original, divine plan. God didn't design the world to have illness or natural disasters.

But through free will, humans brought sin into the world (Romans 5:12). Sin made the world broken, and this brokenness introduced all kinds of human suffering, like cancer, hurricanes, or famines. God feels just as sad about this suffering as your child does because he never intended for people to suffer. In fact, he suffers alongside your child and bears our suffering (Isaiah 53:4-5). He longs to comfort your child. And he promises to make something beautiful out of the broken pieces (Romans 8:28).

Notes

Chapter 5: The Really Big Feelings

1. See Elisabeth Kübler-Ross, *On Death & Dying* (New York: Macmillan, 1969).

Chapter 8: Saying Goodbye to Someone Special

1. See Kenneth Kaufman and Nathaniel Kaufman, "And Then the Dog Died," *Death Studies* 30, no. 1 (2006): 61–76.
2. See "Children and Grief Statistics," ChildrensGriefAwarenessDay.com, https://www.childrensgriefawarenessday.org/cgad2/pdf/griefstatistics.pdf; "Mortality: Adolescents & Young Adults," National Adolescent Health Information Center, http://nahic.ucsf.edu/downloads/Mortality.pdf.
3. See Eva Essa and Coleen Murray, "Death of a Friend," *Childhood Education* 71, no. 3 (1995): 130–34.

Chapter 10: Remembering

1. Emma L. Logan, Jennifer A. Thornton, Robert T. Kane, and Lauren J. Breen, "Social Support Following Bereavement: The Role of Beliefs, Expectations, and Support Intentions," *Death Studies* 42, no. 8 (2018): 471–82.

Chapter 11: The Loss of a Parent

1. See "Number of Children Living with a Single Mother or Single Father in the U.S. from 1970 to 2017 (in 1,000)," Statista, https://www.statista.com/statistics/252847/number-of-children-living-with-a-single-mother-or-single-father/; "Did You Know?: Children and Grief Statistics," Children's Grief Awareness Day, https://www.childrensgriefawarenessday.org/cgad2/pdf/griefstatistics.pdf.
2. Kristin Turney and Christopher Wildeman, "Adverse Childhood Experiences Among Children Placed in and Adopted from Foster Care: Evidence from a Nationally Representative Survey," *Child Abuse & Neglect* 64 (2017): 117–29.
3. See U.S. Census Bureau (2010) statistics at https://www.census.gov/schools/resources/news/fathers.html; see also Irene S. McClatchey, "Fathers Raising Motherless Children: Widowed Men Give Voice to Their Lived Experiences," *OMEGA: Journal of Death and Dying* 76, no. 4 (2018): 307–27.
4. W. Furman, "Children's Patterns in Mourning the Death of a Loved One," *Issues in Comprehensive Pediatric Nursing* 8, no. 1–6 (1985): 185–203.
5. Evangelica Karydi, "Childhood Bereavement: The Role of the Surviving Parent and the Continuing Bond with the Deceased," *Death Studies* 42, no. 7 (2017): 415–25.

Chapter 12: The Death or Disability of a Sibling

1. Wendy Packman, Heidi Horsley, Betty Davies, and Robin Kramer, "Sibling Bereavement and Continuing Bonds," *Death Studies* 30, no. 9 (2006): 817–41.

Chapter 13: The Loss of a Family

1. See "Family Structure and Children's Living Arrangements," ChildStats.gov, https://www.childstats.gov/americaschildren/tables/fam1a.asp.

2. Barbara Jo Fidler and Nicholas Bala, "Children Resisting Postseparation Contact with a Parent: Concepts, Controversies, and Conundrums," *Family Court Review* 48, no. 1 (2010): 10–47.

3. "The AFCARS Report," US Department of Health and Human Services, Administration for Children and Families, Administration on Children, Youth and Families, https://www.acf.hhs.gov/sites/default/files/cb/afcarsreport23.pdf.

4. David J. Schonfeld and Thomas Demaria, "Supporting the Grieving Child and Family," *Pediatrics* 138, no. 3 (September 2016): http://pediatrics.aappublications.org/content/early/2016/08/25/peds.2016-2147.

Chapter 16: Great Will Be Your Children's Peace

1. This verse is speaking about the nation of Israel, but the cultural context refers to a loving father who adores his child.

About the Author

Amy E. Ford, PhD, is a licensed mental health counselor and a university professor. Her counseling practice focuses on trauma, grief, adjustment, and holistic wellness. Amy volunteers as a court-appointed special advocate, supporting children in foster care. She is married to her best friend, Leif, a pastor. Amy and Leif are active in church and community ministry, and they have parented six children together. Amy blogs at authoramyford.com.

To learn more about Harvest House books and to read sample chapters, visit our website:

www.harvesthousepublishers.com